The BUMS Club – Do You Believe It?

Jerry Ascher

First Published - 2024

ISBN 978-1-7337438-2-2

Copyright © TXu 2-399-301 [Jerry Ascher] [2023]

This book is a work of nonfiction. Although the author has made every effort to ensure that the information in this book was correct at press time and while this publication is designed to provide accurate information in regard to the subject matter covered, the author assumes no responsibility for errors, inaccuracies, omissions, or any other inconsistencies herein and hereby disclaims any liability to any party for any loss, damage, or disruption caused by errors or omissions, whether such errors or omissions result from negligence, accident, or any other cause.

Copyright TXu 2-399-301 - All rights reserved.

No part of this publication may be reproduced, stored in or introduced into a retrieval system, or transmitted, in any form, or by any means (electrical, mechanical, photocopying, recording or otherwise) without the prior written permission of the publisher.

Any person who does any unauthorized act in relation to this publication may be liable to criminal prosecution and civil claims for damages.

"THE BUMS CLUB" IS DEDICATED TO THE KIDS I KNEW THAT WALKED FIVE T0 TEN BLOCKS TO GET TO JUNIOR HIGH SCHOOL 50. AFTER YEARS OF WALKING ONLY A FEW BLOCKS TO PUBLIC SCHOOL 16 OR PUBLIC SCHOOL 19, IT WAS A FIVE TO TEN BLOCK WALK FOR THEM TO JUNIOR HIGH SCHOOL 50. THESE KIDS WALKED TO JOHN D. WELLS J.H.S. 50 AND THEN BACK HOME, IN ALL KINDS OF WEATHER.

# Foreword

This book is the story about a group of people who, five days each week from September through June, walked into a building on the corner of South $3^{rd}$ Street and Driggs Avenue in the Williamsburg section of Brooklyn. Above the main entrance to this building is chiseled the words "John D. Wells J H S". Upon entering this building, these folks assumed their positions as members of the faculty of a school which was designated by the NYC Board of Education as Junior High School 50.

For six hours each day this group of people strove to the best of their abilities to provide an education to the students in their charge. It was a challenging job. The teachers in "50", as the school was informally called, faced all of the challenges encountered by countless other teachers in inner city schools. But these dedicated men and women persevered in order to transmit to their students knowledge of subjects such as science, math, social studies, and English. There were many frustrations, but also many rewards.

These people, the faculty of "50", were ordinary people. They lived in ordinary homes, drove ordinary cars, experienced ordinary pleasures, and endured ordinary sorrows. Yet upon entering "50", a group of them coalesced into an organization that was far from ordinary – in fact it was extraordinary. This organization was known as the BUMS Club.

What was the BUMS Club? We can answer this question in part by stating what it was not. It had no written charter, no regular meetings, no dues, and no formal slate of officers, with the exception of a president. The president, who was elected once a year in a carnival atmosphere, had no function other than to arrange periodic bagel parties.

The members of this fine organization hung out in the second-floor teachers' room, known as the BUMS room. This room had little in the way of furnishings to distinguish it from the thousands of other teachers' rooms throughout the NYC school system. There were two tables -- the main function of the smaller one being to hold a coffee pot. There was a couch, always occupied by someone using their free period to catch up on sleep. There were a number of mismatched chairs lining the walls. There was a bulletin board on one of the walls. And there was a bathroom attached to this room.

However, knowing what the BUMS club was not and where its members hung out still does not answer the question of what the BUMS club was and why it was so extraordinary. We first have to answer the question of what the acronym BUMS represents. There are those who say that it stands for "Bring Up Moral Standards." Others say that it stands for "Banish Useless Materials from Schools." Still others say it stands for both.
So we know what the BUMS club was not, where its members hung out, and what the acronym BUMS stands for. Yet this still does not tell you anything about the purpose of this organization.

In essence, the BUMS Club was a means of coping with the stresses that teachers all over the world face in the classroom. Different people cope with stress in different ways. The BUMS Club helped its members deal with stress via the mechanism of humor and outlandish behavior. No matter how down a teacher felt, within five minutes of entering the BUMS room he was convulsed with laughter. In the BUMS room you could get the answer to any question you had. Sometimes, the answer might even be correct. You could also get advice on how to handle any problem, whether or not you wanted this advice.

The BUMS Club was analogous to the group of surgeons in the movie/TV series MASH, who dealt with the carnage they witnessed on a daily basis by participating in various outlandish activities. And similar to their MASH counterparts, the BUMS quickly whittled down to size anyone demonstrating pomposity or self importance.

I became quite excited when Jerry told me of his plans to write this book. By committing to paper the exploits and anecdotes of the BUMS of "50", this book bestows upon them a degree of immortality. In the decades to come, as long as one copy of this book remains gathering dust on a bookshelf, in a storage bin, in a basement, or in an attic, the story of this remarkable group of people will lie in hibernation, ready to spring to life the moment the book is opened by some future reader.

This book is the story of a group of ordinary people who worked in a building on the corner of South 3rd Street and Driggs Avenue. It is the story of how they coped with the frustrations inherent in their jobs. What's more, it is the story of people I was privileged to be friends with. Hopefully, this book will bring back pleasant memories and chuckles to those BUMS still alive and serve as a memorial to those who have passed.

By Sholom Schwartz

# TABLE OF CONTENTS      "THE BUMS CLUB"

**"THE BUMS CLUB"**                                pg 1

**BUMS GROUP 1==**
**INTRODUCING SOME BUMS**          pg 7
THE NEIGHBORHOOD                   pg 15
DISTRICT SUPERINTENDANT JOINS
THE BUMS CLUB                      pg 18

**BUMS GROUP 2==**
**MORE TERRIFIC BUMS**             pg 20
NEIGHBORHOOD STORES                pg 27

**BUMS GROUP 3==**
**SOME MORE BUMS**                 pg 31
HOMEROOM AND QUOTA TEACHERS        pg 36
ATTENDANCE IMPROVEMENT
DROPOUT PREVENTION                 pg 37

**BUMS GROUP 4==**
**THE BUMS KEEP COMING**           pg 40
VACATION DAY CAMP
SUMMER PROGRAM                     pg 45

**BUMS GROUP 5==**
**SOME WINNING BUMS**              pg 49
THE TEACHER TALENT SHOW,
ABOVE AND BEYOND                   pg 56

**BUMS GROUP 6==**
**BUMS, BUMS, BUMS**               pg 58
BUMS SOCIALIZING                   pg 64
BUMS ROOM GUESTS, STORIES
AND MORE                           pg 68
THE BUMS, TRYING TO REMEMBER
THEM ALL                           pg 75

| | |
|---|---|
| THE BUMS ROOM HAD IT ALL | pg 82 |
| DISTRICT 14 IN THE NEWS | pg 85 |
| BUMS ARE REMEMBERED, TAKE A BOW | pg 91 |
| A SCHOOL FOR GENERATIONS | pg 100 |
| WILL THE BUMS HAVE A 50 YEAR REUNION? | pg 102 |
| THE SUMMARY | pg 118 |

**TABLE OF BUMS**
**NO FULL NAMES TO PROTECT THE GUILTY**

**BUMS GROUP 1==**
**INTRODUCING SOME BUMS** pg 7

- **DEAN SAM** - CHAINED HOUSE BURGLAR, PIPE IN DESK
- **MR. SAM 1** - FAKE COVERAGE SLIP
- **MR. MARV** - AVOIDED THE ASSISSTANT PRINCIPAL TO GET SNACKS
- **MR. AL 1** - ONLY THE EXTENSION CORD WAS RETURNED
- **MR. AL 2** - THE CHAIRMAN SIGN SCREWED UPSIDE DOWN
- **BOSS GENE** - COFFEE CLUB AND END OF MONTH LUNCH
- **MR. VINNY** – PRANKOLOGIST, CORD AND SIGN
- **MR. WARREN** – PRANKERER, THE WHITE SHADOW, VICE RAID HEADLINE

**BUMS GROUP 2==**
**MORE TERRIFIC BUMS** pg 20

- **MR. STANLEY** - JUST WRITE ANYTHING, DID THE MONKEY
- **MR. SAM 1** - $2^{ND}$ TIME, HUGGED THE READING TEACHER
- **MR. BEN 1** - THE SECRETARY'S DESK, HE CARRIED HER UP THE STAIRS

- MR. JERRY – PRANKIST, RED B FOR GRAPH PAPER PRANK
- MR. DICK - TIE BURNING INITIATION, ONLY PLAYED 2 CHORDS
- MR. JOHN – PRANKPRO, SHOPPING CART ON DISPLAY
- MR. AL 3 - THE DRUMMER, EVERYONE EXCEPT YOU
- MR. BARRY - A LAWYER, WENT TO COURT FOR A BUM

**BUMS GROUP 3==**
**SOME MORE BUMS**                                pg 31
- MR. PETE 1 - G.O. BUTTONS, G.O. MOVIE, 2 BOOKS OF STAMPS
- MR. SAM 1 - 3$^{RD}$ TIME, USE OTHER DOOR, 20/20 OR 40/40
- MR. BEN 2 - NOISY CLASS HAS A GOOD POINT
- MR. ARTIE 1 - SHOESHINE BOX TEACHING
- MR. ROBERT 1 - MEMORY COURSE
- MR. MARK - BUMS ROOM BLOOD TECHNICIAN
- MR. NEFTI - FRONT PAGE NEWS

**BUMS GROUP 4==**
**THE BUMS KEEP COMING**                    pg 40
- ASSISTANT PRINCIPAL BERNIE - NOSE AND TOES
- MR. WARREN – PRANKERER, 2$^{ND}$ TIME, ARISTA NOMINEES, BIG BELT
- MR. JOHN – PRANKPRO, 2$^{ND}$ TIME, THE STOCKBROKER
- MR. WILLIAM - AREA POLITICS
- MR. AL 3 - 2$^{ND}$ TIME, 3 MILE ISLAND EGGS
- MR. MARV - 2$^{ND}$ TIME, TAKING A SHAVE WITH PRINCIPAL
- MR. LESTER - NO OPEN WINDOW REPAIRS

**BUMS GROUP 5==**
**SOME WINNING BUMS**                          pg 49
- **MR. S.** – PRANKWRITER, DISTRICT SUP APPLICATION, SUPPLY FORM
- **MR. SAM 1** - 4$^{TH}$ TIME, CHICKENS 51 CENTS A POUND
- **MR. JOE 1** - EARLY IN, EARLY OUT
- **MR. LENNY 1** - 3 CHERRIES, CLASS VERY QUIET
- **MR. MARV** - 3$^{RD}$ TIME, HOT CHERRY PEPPERS
- **MR. WARREN** – PRANKERER, 3$^{RD}$ TIME, JIGSAW PUZZLE SHIRT
- **DR. SAM** - SONG AND DANCE MAN

**BUMS GROUP 6==**
**BUMS, BUMS, BUMS**                           pg 58
- **PRINCIPAL** FRANK -POKER, MATCHES, ARSENIC AND OLD LACE
- **MR. MARIO** - HELPED THEM STAY AT 50
- **MR. GIL** - FIRST BUMS BASH
- **MR. PETE 1** - 2$^{ND}$ TIME, ON THE WALL, TANK POSTER, PRINCIPAL EYE CHART
- **MR. ROBERT 2** - LOOK AT MOM WALK
- **DEAN SAM** - 2$^{ND}$ TIME, HAD A PADDLE
- **MR. PHIL** - COME AS YOU ARE
- **MR. MEL** - GREAT BUM PARTICIPATOR, BUM PIN IDEA, FILM DIRECTOR
- **MISS MARIE** - CRIED AT THE CEREMONY

**THE BUMS==TRYING TO REMEMBER THEM ALL**
- THERE ARE MORE THAN 50 NAMES

**BUMS ARE REMEMBERED=TAKE A BOW**
- MANY BUMS ARE REMEMBERED BY THE STUDENTS

"THE BUMS CLUB"

THIS BOOK CONTAINS THE MEMORIES OF MANY TEACHERS THAT SPENT FIFTEEN YEARS OR MORE TEACHING AT JUNIOR HIGH SCHOOL 50 IN THE WILLIAMSBURG SECTION OF BROOKLYN. WHEN NOT IN THE CLASSROOM THEY GATHERED IN THE SECOND FLOOR TEACHERS' LOUNGE WHICH WAS TO BE CALLED "THE BUMS ROOM". THESE GUYS SPENT HOURS BEING ENTERTAINED AND UNWINDING IN THAT BUMS ROOM. SINCE RETIRING MANY OF THE BUMS STAYED CONNECTED TALKING ON THE PHONE AND SOCIALIZING WITH EACH OTHER IN VARIOUS SIZE GROUPS. NO MATTER WHERE OR HOW WE WERE TOGETHER, THE CONVERSATION STEERED TO MANY INDIVIDUAL BUMS, THEIR ANTICS AND PERSONALITIES. DURING EVERY CONVERSATION ONE OF US WOULD BLURT OUT, THERE SHOULD BE A BOOK ABOUT THE BUMS ROOM, BUT WHO'S GONNA BELIEVE IT? SO HERE I AM WRITING THE BOOK WITH THE THOUGHTS AND MEMORIES OF SOME OF MY FELLOW BUMS. WE WERE SORT OF PROUD TO BE CALLED BUMS.

I WRITE A SHORT DESCRIPTION OF EACH BUM FOLLOWED BY SOME ACTIVITY, ANTIC OR EVENT THAT QUALIFIED HIM FOR BUMDOM. ACTUALLY, IT WAS SOMETHING IN EACH GUYS PERSONALITY THAT GUIDED HIM INTO THE BUMS CLUB. YOU WILL BE INTRODUCED TO MORE THAN THIRTY BUMS, SOME APPEARING MANY TIMES. ALSO, THERE WILL BE STORIES OF BUMS ROOM VISITORS WHO COULD HAVE BEEN BUMS IF THEY SPENT MORE TIME IN THE BUMS ROOM. THROUGHOUT THE BOOK THERE WILL BE STORIES ABOUT THE BUMS CLUB MEMBERS. THE MEMBERS WERE SEASONED OR NEWER TEACHERS, ALL MALE, THAT ENJOYED THE CAMARADERIE,

CONVERSATION, KIDDING, HUMOR, OPINIONS, SARCASM AND FUN IN THAT SMALL, CROWDED TEACHERS' ROOM.

BECAUSE THERE WERE BUMS WITH THE SAME NAMES (MR. AL, MR. SAM, MR. BEN, MR. ROBERT, MR. PETE), A NUMBER WAS ASSIGNED TO EACH BUM TO DISTINGUISH THEM FROM EACH OTHER IN THE STORIES. MR. AL 1, MR. AL 2, MR. AL 3, ALL VERY DIFFERENT!!

WHEN I GOT TO THIS SCHOOL THERE WAS A FIRST TIME PRINCIPAL, A WWII HERO, A PLEASANT GENTLEMAN. THE PRINCIPAL BEFORE HIM TRANSFERRED TO ANOTHER SCHOOL IN BROOKLYN, TAKING MANY STAFF MEMBERS WITH HIM. THIS NEW PRINCIPAL HAD TO HIRE MANY TEACHERS TO FILL THE POSITIONS. I HAD A MATH LICENSE WHICH MADE HIM HAPPY TO ADD ME TO HIS MATH DEPARTMENT. WHEN THE TERM BEGAN MANY NEW TEACHERS CONGREGATED IN THE SECOND FLOOR TEACHERS' ROOM WHICH WAS ON THE SAME FLOOR AS THE MAIN OFFICE. AFTER CLOCKING IN, THE TEACHERS HAD SOME TIME TO CHAT. SOME WENT TO THE LIBRARY, SOME TO AN EMPTY CLASSROOM, WHILE A GROUP OF FEMALE TEACHERS MET IN THE COOKING SHOP CLASSROOM. I LIKED THE $2^{nd}$ FLOOR TEACHERS' ROOM NEAR THE MAIN OFFICE.

BUMS Room Lunch

THE SECOND FLOOR TEACHERS' "LOUNGE" BECAME POPULAR TO A NICE GROUP OF GUYS. BECAUSE THE SAME GROUP OF GUYS FREQUENTED THE 2nd FLOOR "LOUNGE" A FEW SUGGESTED THAT WE HAVE A HOLIDAY SOCIAL OUTSIDE THE SCHOOL. MR. GIL AND MR. JERRY TOOK ON THE CHORE OF FINDING A PLACE FOR A PARTY. A QUESTION CAME UP. WHAT IS THE NAME OF OUR GROUP?

WHEN STUDENT MONITORS WERE SENT TO THE SECOND FLOOR TEACHERS' ROOM, THEY GOT A VIEW OF A DISORDERLY ROOM WITH TEACHERS SLEEPING ON MARKED UP CHAIRS AND THE OLD DISCOLORED, SUNKEN IN COT. A COUPLE OF PARENTS WERE TOLD THERE WERE BUMS SLEEPING IN THAT ROOM. THE ROOM GOT THE NAME "THE BUMS ROOM". IT WAS SUGGESTED THAT WE BE CALLED THE BUMS CLUB. BUMS STANDING FOR Bring Up Moral Standards.

WHEN WE AGREED THAT WE ARE THE BUMS CLUB, IT WAS RECOMENDED THAT WE HAVE OFFICERS. THE CONCENSUS WAS THAT WE HAVE ONLY ONE OFFICE, THE PRESIDENT. THERE WAS NO ELECTION. IT WAS AGREED THAT MR. VINNY SHOULD BE PRESIDENT. MR. VINNY WAS LIVELY, A GREAT STORYTELLER AND ALWAYS ATTRACTED ATTENTION.

THE BUMS CLUB WAS FORMED AND HAD THEIR FIRST SOCIAL AT A CATERING HALL IN QUEENS, N.Y. BECAUSE OF A MR. MEL IDEA, GOLD BUM PINS WERE ORDERED AND DISTRIBUTED TO EACH MEMBER. WIVES, FRIENDS AND OTHER STAFF MEMBERS, THAT WERE NOT PART OF THE BUMS CLUB, ASKED TO BE INVITED TO THE BUMS BASH. ONE HUNDRED PEOPLE ATTENDED INCLUDING AN ASSISTANT PRINCIPAL AND ONE OF THE SENIOR TEACHERS IN THE SCHOOL. THIS EVENT WAS A SUCCESSFUL KICKOFF FOR THE BUMS CLUB.

BUMS BASH

WHEN ENTERING THE BUMS ROOM, TEACHERS WOULD THROW THEIR BELONGINGS ON A CHAIR, A LITTLE DESK OR THE BIG TABLE IN THE CENTER OF THE ROOM. COFFEE CLUB MEMBERS WOULD GET COFFEE WHICH WAS ON A TABLE NEXT TO THE DOOR. DIRECTLY ACROSS THE ROOM, OPPOSITE THE DOOR WERE TWO WINDOWS FACING THE STREET. IN THE RIGHT CORNER OF THIS ROOM NEXT TO THE WINDOW WAS A SMALL BATHROOM. THIS ROOM WAS NOT TREATED LIKE THE NORMAL TEACHERS' LOUNGE. IT WAS MORE LIKE A CLUBROOM. IF YOU WANTED A QUIET ATMOSPHERE, YOU WENT ELSEWHERE. IF YOU WANTED LOUD CONVERSATION, ENTER AT YOUR OWN RISK.

THE BUMS ROOM RESEMBLED A TELEVISION SITCOM LIKE BARNEY MILLER, TAXI, OR SOME OTHER T.V. SITCOMS THAT HAD DISTINCT CHARACTERS. THE BUMS ROOM HAD MORE THAN ONE OF EACH KIND. THE INTELLECTUAL TYPE ADMIRED FOR HIS KNOWLEDGE, THE BETTER DRESSED GUY WHOSE CLOTHES WERE WONDERFULLY MATCHED, LOOKING FRESH WITH NO STAINS, THE GUY WHOSE JACKET LOOKED AS IF HE SLEPT IN IT BECAUSE HE DID AND THE GUY THAT WAS CONSIDERED MUCH LESS INTELLIGENT THAN THE REST OF THE GROUP. THERE WERE OLDER GUYS ALWAYS GRUMPY. THERE WAS THE GAMBLER, LOOKING TO MAKE A BET ON ANYTHING AND THE BORN VICTIM BECAUSE EVERYTHING HAPPENS TO THIS GUY. THE BUMS ROOM HAD ITS SITCOM OF CHARACTERS.

THERE WILL BE GROUPS OF BUMS PRESENTED THROUGHOUT THE BOOK WITH A MINI PROFILE FOR EACH, GIVING SOME IDEA OF THE PERSON. IT WILL BE FOLLOWED BY AN ACTIVITY OR EVENT INVOLVING

THE BUM. THERE WILL BE NO FULL NAMES TO AVOID UNEASINESS OR EMBARRASSMENT.
THE BOOK INCLUDES A DESCRIPTION OF THE NEIGHBORHOOD, THE FRIENDLY STORES IN THE AREA, SCHOOL PROGRAMS, AND MOST IMPORTANT THE RESPONSES FROM THE STUDENTS ON THE INTERNET SHOWING THEIR FEELINGS, THOUGHTS AND MEMORIES OF JUNIOR HIGH SCHOOL 50 AND THEIR TEACHERS OF THIRTY TO FIFTY YEARS AGO.

## BUMS GROUP 1===INTRODUCING SOME BUMS

*NO FULL NAMES TO PROTECT THE GUILTY.*

THIS IS A GROUP OF POSSIBLE SITCOM CHARACTERS. YOU WILL BE INTRODUCED TO EIGHT BUMS. ONE DOES NOT TAKE CRAP FROM ANYONE, ANOTHER WHO GETS CRAP FROM EVERYONE. A GUY THAT WILL BET ON ANYTHING AND AN OLD GRUMPY GUY IN HIS OLD WRINKLED SUIT. ONE GUY WHO DOESN'T SEEM TO CARE AND ONE THAT LIKES TO BE IN CHARGE. HERE COMES THE FIRST GROUP OF BUMS.

DEAN SAM===WELL DRESSED, BIG, STRONG, INTIMIDATING, TOUGH REPUTATION==EXTREMELY HELPFUL TO STAFF, FRIENDLY AND JOVIAL==DID NOT SPEND MUCH TIME IN THE BUMS ROOM, HE LIKED HIS DEAN'S OFFICE==HE BECAME A JUNIOR HIGH SCHOOL 50 LEGEND. STORIES ABOUT HIM AND FROM HIM MADE US THINK OF HIM AS OUR JOHN HENRY, OUR FOLKTALE HERO.

DEAN SAM TELLS THE STORY ABOUT TWO GUYS BURGLARIZING HIS HOUSE. DEAN SAM SPENT TIME IN BARS IN HIS NEIGHBORHOOD. HE SOUGHT OUT THE TWO THAT DID THE ROBBERY. WHEN HE GOT HOLD OF ONE, HE TOOK THE BURGLAR TO HIS HOUSE AND CHAINED HIM TO SUPPORTING PIPES IN HIS BASEMENT. DEAN SAM FED HIM BREAD AND WATER. WHEN THE MISSING STUFF WAS RETURNED THE BURGLAR WAS RELEASED. THIS WAS A HARD STORY TO ACCEPT UNTIL MEETING HIS NEIGHBOR WHO EXPLAINED EXACTLY THE WAY HE SAW THE GUY CHAINED TO THE PIPES. THE NEIGHBOR CONFIRMED THE STORY.

A YOUNG SCIENCE TEACHER WAS HAVING A TOUGH TIME IN HER HOMEROOM WITH A 9th GRADE STUDENT. SHE SPOKE TO DEAN SAM ABOUT THE PROBLEM. THE DEAN KNEW ABOUT THIS STUDENT, SO HE PUT A PLAN INTO ACTION. AFTER HE WAS SHOWN THE POSITION OF THE STUDENT'S DESK, DEAN SAM PLACED A LEAD PIPE IN THE STUDENT'S DESK EARLY THAT MORNING. WHEN THE STUDENT WAS SITTING AT HIS DESK DURING HOMEROOM, DEAN SAM CAME INTO THE ROOM, LOOKED IN THE DESK AND TOOK THE STUDENT WITH THE PIPE DOWN TO THE DEAN'S OFFICE. DEAN SAM GAVE THE KID SOME CHOICES. THE STUDENT WAS NOT A WISE ASS WITH THAT TEACHER ANYMORE.

MR. SAM 1---THE BORN VICTIM—ALWAYS HAVING TROUBLE—HE HAD TROUBLE WITH NEIGHBORS, DENTIST, FAMILY AND SOCIETY IN GENERAL.

IN THE BUMS ROOM HE TOLD US THAT HIS DENTIST PULLED THE WRONG TOOTH.
THE BUMS ROOM HAD ITS MORNING CROWD. A MONITOR KNOCKED ON THE DOOR THEN GAVE MR. SAM 1 A COVERAGE SLIP. A COVERAGE SLIP IS AN ASSIGNMENT TO TAKE A CLASS WHEN THE TEACHER IS NOT AVAILABLE. TEACHERS ARE PAID FOR THESE COVERAGES AT THE END OF THE MONTH. WHEN IT WAS PAYDAY, MR. SAM 1 ASKED THE COVERAGE COORDINATOR WHY HE DIDN'T GET PAID FOR THAT COVERAGE? HE WAS TOLD THAT IT WAS NOT AUTHORIZED, IT DID NOT COME FROM THE OFFICE. THERE WAS NO RECORD OF THAT COVERAGE. SOMEONE PRANKED HIM. THIS CAUSED MR. SAM 1 TO DO A HANDWRITING INVESTIGATION OF THOSE HE SUSPECTED OF THE PRANK.

MR. MARV===COLLEGE BASEBALL PLAYER==TOUGH BUILD, TOUGH LOOK, TOUGH TALK, PUTS YOU DOWN TALK==LIKES TO DISCUSS SPORTS==READS A WEEKLY SPORTS PUBLICATION==LIKES A GOOD BET

MR. MARV MIGHT BE THE FIRST ONE IN THE BUMS ROOM EVERY MORNING. HIS BARTENDING JOB KEPT HIM OUT TOO LATE FOR HIM TO GO HOME. HE FELT THAT HE'D DO BETTER BY WAITING FOR THE CUSTODIAL STAFF TO OPEN THE SCHOOL SO HE COULD GET COZY ON THE OLD DISCOLORED COT, TO GET AN HOUR OR TWO OF SLEEP. HE HAD A CLASS OF SPECIAL NEEDS STUDENTS. THEY REMAINED IN HIS CLASSROOM MOST OF THE DAY. HE LIKED TO TREAT THEM TO SNACKS EVERYDAY. HE WOULD SEND ONE OF HIS STUDENTS ACROSS THE STREET TO THE BODEGA TO BUY TREATS FOR THE CLASS. HIS SUPERVISOR WAS 100% AGAINST THIS AND LET HIM KNOW THAT HE WILL STOP THE STUDENT FROM LEAVING THE BUILDING. BECAUSE THE SUPERVISOR INTERCEPTED THE STUDENT, MR. MARV STARTED SENDING TWO STUDENTS IN DIFFERENT DIRECTIONS TO BRING BACK THE DONUTS AND CHIPS. THE KIDS LOVED THE GAME, DODGING ASSISTANT PRINCIPAL PHIL AND BEING THE ONE TO BRING BACK THE DONUTS.

MR. AL 1===TIRED==SOLD INSURANCE==LOVED THE COT==WRINKLED SUIT JACKET, GREY HAIR MOSTLY GONE, THE REST OF HIS HAIR READY TO BE COMBED==CONFUSED ABOUT THE PUBLIC SCHOOL SYSTEM==LIKED THE BUMS, ONE OF THE REASONS WAS THEY WOKE HIM WHEN IT WAS TIME TO GO TO CLASS.

MR. AL 1 WAS KNOWN FOR THREE THINGS, ENJOYING A NAP, HAVING AN OLD CAR AND ALWAYS HAVING

SCREWDRIVERS IN HIS JACKET POCKET. HE WAS AN OFFICER IN A FRATERNITY WHICH HAD HIM DRIVING TO COLLEGES TO MEET WITH THE YOUNGER FRAT BROTHERS. OFTEN, HE WOULD RETURN HOME VERY LATE AT NIGHT. IF HIS OLD CAR BROKEDOWN HE WOULD USE HIS SCREWDRIVERS TO REMOVE HIS LICENSE PLATES. HE'D ABANDON THE CAR AND GET ANOTHER OLD CAR. MR. AL 1 WAS AN INTERESTING BUMS ROOM CHARACTER WHEN HE DIDN'T NEED SLEEP.

MR. AL 1 TAUGHT SOCIAL STUDIES. AT TIMES SCHOOL BUSINESS WAS CONDUCTED IN THE BUMS ROOM. THIS MORNING MR. AL 2 THE SOCIAL STUDIES CHAIRMAN WAS IN THE BUMS ROOM. MR. AL 1 ASKED THE CHAIRMAN FOR A SLIDE PROJECTOR, SLIDES, EXTENSION CORD AND THE REST OF THE STUFF. MR. AL 2 REQUESTED THAT ALL OF IT BE RETURNED BEFORE THE END OF THE DAY. MR. JERRY AND MR. VINNY HEARD THE CONVERSATION. WHEN THEY WERE IN THE BUMS ROOM NEAR THE END OF THE DAY, MR. VINNY AND MR. JERRY SENT TWO MONITORS WITH A NOTE TO MR. AL 1 REQUESTING THE PROJECTOR AND THE REST OF THE STUFF TO BE RETURNED WITH THE TWO MONITORS. ALL WAS RETURNED TO MR. VINNY AND MR. JERRY IN THE BUMS ROOM. MR. JERRY AND MR. VINNY PROMTLY RETURNED ONLY THE EXTENSION CORD TO MR. AL 2 THE SOCIAL STUDIES CHAIRMAN. THE TWO THOUGHT THIS WAS A CUTE PRANK. AT THE TIMECLOCK MR. AL 2 APPROACHED MR. AL 1 ASKING FOR THE SLIDES AND PROJECTOR. MR. AL 1 TRIED TO EXPLAIN THAT HE SENT EVERYTHING TO HIM WITH HIS TWO MONITORS. ALL WAS DELIVERED TO OUR SOCIAL STUDIES CHAIRMAN THE NEXT MORNING. MR. AL 1 SMILED WHEN HE KNEW WHO DID THE PRANKING.

MR. AL 2===VERY SERIOUS ABOUT BEING SOCIAL STUDIES CHAIRMAN AND ALSO LATER AS BUMS PRESIDENT==NOT KNOWN FOR HUMOR==DRESSED ACCORDING TO THE COUNTRY OF THE LESSON==STUDENTS RESPECTED HIS TEACHING METHODS.

MR. AL 2 WANTED RESPECT FOR HIS CHAIRMAN POSITION. HE HUNG A WOODEN SIGN ON HIS DOOR WITH HIS NAME AND THE TITLE SOCIAL STUDIES CHAIRMAN. MR. VINNY AND BOSS GENE REMOVED IT AND SCREWED IT ONTO HIS DOOR UPSIDE DOWN.

BOSS GENE===WAY ABOVE AVERAGE HEIGHT==TAKE CHARGE GUY==BUMS CLUB EVENT COORDINATOR==BUMS ROOM CONTRIBUTOR, OPINIONATED, CONTROVERSIAL==PLENTY TO SAY==COMPETENT WITH TOOLS.

HE REVERSED THE CHAIRMAN SIGN IN RECORD TIME. BOSS GENE AND A FEW GUYS WOULD USUALLY ARRIVE TO THE BUMS ROOM AN HOUR BEFORE THE START OF THE SCHOOL DAY. OTHERS WOULD DRIFT IN A FEW AT A TIME. MANY MORNINGS WHEN THEY ENTERED THE BUMS ROOM MR. MARV WAS SLEEPING ON THE OLD DUSTY COT, SHOES ON AND JACKET COVERING HIS HEAD. BOSS GENE WOULD TRY TO BE QUIET SO MR. MARV COULD GET MORE SLEEP WHILE BOSS GENE PREPARED THE COFFEE.

BOSS GENE COLLECTED MONEY MONTHLY FROM THE BUMS THAT WANTED TO BE IN THE COFFEE CLUB. AT THE END OF THE MONTH, WITH THE REMAINING MONEY, THE BOSS AND A COUPLE OF RECRUITS WOULD GO OUT IN THE NEIGHBORHOOD TO GET THE FOOD FOR A BUMS' LUNCH. A FEW BLOCKS AWAY WAS THE POLISH BAKERY FOR FRESH DELICIOUS RYE

BREAD, KOSHER SALAMI WAS GOTTEN AT THE FACTORY, SO WITH PICKLES, MUSTARD AND THE REST, THE BUMS HAD A GREAT END OF MONTH LUNCH IN THE BUMS ROOM. MR. DON SUPPLIED A GALLON OF HOMEMADE WINE FROM HIS DAD'S WINE CELLAR.

MR. VINNY===PRANKOLOGIST==FIRST BUMS PRESIDENT==LIVELY—LIFE OF THE BUMS ROOM==BUMS ROOM CONTRIBUTOR SUPREME==ATTENTION GETTING CONVERSATIONALIST==STUDENTS' FAVORITE.

MR. VINNY WAS INVOLVED IN MANY GREAT PRANKS LIKE INTERCEPTING ALL THE AUDIO=VISUAL EQUIPMENT AND RETURNING ONLY THE EXTENSION CORD TO THE SOCIAL STUDIES CHAIRMAN. TURNING THE SOCIAL STUDIES CHAIRMAN DOOR SIGN UPSIDE DOWN. THERE'S MORE TO COME.

MR. WARREN===PRANKERER==RELENTLESS==BUMS ROOM CONTRIBUTOR==HUMOROUS IDEAS==SCHOOL TRIP KING

MR. WARREN WAS KNOWN FOR TAKING CLASSES ON TRIPS TO MANHATTAN. THERE COULD BE 1,2 OR 3 OTHER CLASSES AND TEACHERS WITH HIM. IT WAS USUALLY THE SAME BUMS THAT TOOK THEIR CLASSES WITH THE TRIP KING. THE NEXT DAY THERE WOULD BE GREAT STORIES IN THE BUMS ROOM ABOUT THE TRIP.

OUR BAND AND CHORUS WERE TERRIFIC. MR. EARL LED THE CHORUS AND TAUGHT GENERAL MUSIC. THE MUSIC ROOM HELD TWO FULL CLASSES SO THE MUSIC TEACHER WAS GIVEN ANOTHER TEACHER AS AN ASSISTANT. THE ADMINISTRATION TRIED TO ASSIGN

A TEACHER THAT PLAYED AN INSTRUMENT ALTHOUGH THE ASSISTANT WAS THERE MOSTLY TO TAKE THE ATTENDANCE.
A NEW MUSIC TEACHER, LACKING EVERY QUALIFICATION FOR BEING IN A CLASSROOM, WAS ASSIGNED TO OUR SCHOOL. HE WAS ASKED TO PLAY THE STAR=SPANGLED BANNER IN THE AUDITORIUM, BUT HE REFUSED. HE DID PLAY THE TWO CHORDS FOR THE STUDENTS TO STAND UP AND SIT DOWN. ONE OF BUMS SAID HE'S THE HIGHEST PAID MUSIC TEACHER IN AMERICA. TWO SECONDS WORK WITH FULL SALARY.

IF YOU RECALL THERE WAS A TELEVISION SHOW CALLED "THE WHITE SHADOW", A WHITE COACH WITH BLACK BASKETBALL PLAYERS.
OUR CHORUS TEACHER WAS BLACK AND LED THE CHORUS AT A BLACK CHURCH WHERE HE WAS AFFECTIONATELY CALLED "THE MUSIC MAN". THE NEW MUSIC TEACHER WAS A TALL WHITE, SHLUBBY GUY ALWAYS FOLLOWING THE MUSIC MAN. MR. WARREN GAVE HIM THE NAME "THE WHITE SHADOW"
MR. DICK, KNOWN TO THE BUMS AS THE WHITE SHADOW, LIKED THE ATMOSPHERE OF THE BUMS ROOM. HE LIKED IT SO MUCH HE ASKED TO BE A MEMBER OF THE BUMS CLUB. HE ALWAYS WORE A TIE WITH HALF HIS SHIRT HANGING OUT OF HIS PANTS. LATER WILL COME THE TIE BURNING INITIATION CEREMONY OF MR. DICK, THE WHITE SHADOW.

ASSISTANT PRINCIPAL MISS AUDREY WAS KNOWN AS A PAIN IN THE ASS.
DURING A THREE CLASS TRIP MR. WARREN AND MR. JEFF 1 STOPPED AT A PHONY HEADLINE PRINTING PLACE ON 8th AVENUE IN NEW YORK CITY. THEY HAD

A LARGE HEADLINE PRINTED THAT WAS HUNG HIGH OVER THE DOOR OF THE BUMS ROOM. MR. WARREN AND MR. JEFF 1 HAD PRANKED ASSISTANT PRINCIPAL AUDREY IN THE PAST, BY PUTTING THINGS IN HER MAILBOX, NOTES UNDER HER DOOR AND LITTLE CRITTERS ON HER DESK. MR. WARREN WAS THE SEVENTH GRADE ADVISOR AND HAD AN OFFICE NEXT TO ASSISTANT PRINCIPAL MISS AUDREY. WHENEVER SHE LEFT HER OFFICE, HE LOOKED TO DO SOMETHING THAT WOULD ANNOY HER. THE DAY AFTER THEIR CLASS TRIP, THE HEADLINE WAS HUNG HIGH ABOVE THE DOOR OF THE BUMS ROOM. IT, READ ASSISTANT PRINCIPAL AUDREY CAUGHT NAKED IN VICE RAID WITH MR. DICKIE. SHE REPORTED THIS TO THE DISTRICT SUPERINTENDANT WHO PROBABLY LAUGHED THINKING IT WAS MOST LIKELY DONE BY THE BUMS.

YOU WERE JUST INTRODUCED TO A SAMPLE OF THE GUYS IN THE BUMS CLUB. TOUGH, TIRED, SERIOUS, CREATIVE, TRICKY, SOCIALLY INEPT, HUMOROUS AND WHATEVER ELSE? TEACHERS COME IN ALL TYPES, SIZES AND SHAPES. THERE WILL BE MORE GROUPS OF BUMS WITH THEIR THOUGHTS AND ANTICS. MANY, MANY MORE ARE COMING.

## THE NEIGHBORHOOD

THE STREETS AROUND THE SCHOOL WERE STREWN WITH RUBBISH, GARBAGE, CANS, BOTTLES AND BROKEN GLASS. THERE WERE RUINED BURNTOUT BUILDINGS WITHOUT WINDOWS WITH PEOPLE INSIDE AVOIDING THE WEATHER OUTSIDE. A YOUNG NEIGHBOR OF MINE TOLD ME HE WAS STARTING A JOB AT A CONSTRUCTION SITE IN WILLIAMSBURG. HE WAS HAPPY WHEN I OFFERED TO DRIVE HIM TO THE SITE THE NEXT MORNING. NEXT MORNING DRIVING NEAR JUNIOR HIGH SCHOOL 50 HE SAW PEOPLE STANDING AROUND THE FIRES IN BIG STEEL DRUMS. HE SAW PEOPLE IN THE HOUSES STANDING NEAR THE BROKEN, GLASSLESS WINDOWS. HE ASKED ME "ARE THEY MAKING A MOVIE ON THIS BLOCK?" I SMILED AND TOLD HIM, "YOU ARE SEEING REAL LIFE"

ONE BLOCK FROM THE SCHOOL THERE WAS A LITTLE BODEGA THAT SOLD SOME FRUITS AND VEGETABLES. THE OWNER WAS ANNOYED WHEN BOYS WOULD TAKE FRUIT AND QUICKLY LEAVE WITHOUT PAYING. ONE DAY THE OWNER SHOT A BOY DEAD. LATER THAT DAY HE GOT ON A PLANE AND WENT BACK TO HIS COUNTRY. THAT NIGHT HIS STORE WAS SET ON FIRE AND BURNT TO THE GROUND. DAYS LATER THERE WAS A PARADE PASSING THROUGH THE STREET IN FRONT OF THE SCHOOL IN REMEMBRANCE.

PEOPLE WERE LOOKING TO MOVE OUT OF THIS NEIGHBORHOOD. THERE WERE STREET GANGS. TWO OF THEM WERE CALLED "THE HELL BURNERS" AND "THE PHANTOM LORDS". BEING OUT AT NIGHT WAS NOT SAFE. THE SCHOOL WAS QUITE SAFE. BUT STILL, NOT TOO MANY KIDS TOOK ADVANTAGE OF THE AFTERSCHOOL LEARNING PROGRAMS. JUNIOR HIGH

SCHOOL 50 HAD A HOMEWORK HELPER PROGRAM. MATH AND READING IMPROVEMENT WAS THE FOCUS OF THE AFTERSCHOOL PROGRAMS. A MAJOR ISSUE WAS THE KIDS HAD A SHELTERED LIFE. WHEN ASKED TO NAME AS MANY JOBS OR OCCUPATIONS AS THEY CAN, THEY CAME UP WITH ABOUT TEN JOBS. JUST THE EVERYDAY JOBS WAS IN THEIR VOCABULARY. THE STUDENTS SHOULD BE INTRODUCED TO THE DICTIONARY OF TRADES, THE BOOK WITH 10,000 OCCUPATIONS IN IT.
MANY YOUNGSTERS ALSO WOULD NOT AVAIL THEMSELVES OF THE AFTERSCHOOL RECREATION PROGRAMS OR PLAYING IN THE SCHOOL YARDS. THE RECREATION PROGRAMS WERE MOSTLY USED BY THE NEIGHBORHOOD TOUGHS, ESPECIALLY DURING THE EVENING PROGRAMS. THE SCHOOL WAS KEPT SAFE WHILE THE STREETS HAD ITS PROBLEMS. IN THE THIRTY YEARS THAT I WORKED AT JUNIOR HIGH SCHOOL 50, I'M NOT AWARE OF ANY SHOOTING OR STABBING IN THE SCHOOL. THE PARENTS HAD GREAT RESPECT FOR THE TEACHERS. THIS PHRASE WAS DISPLAYED ON THE BUMS ROOM WALL BECAUSE OF THE TIMES A PARENT WOULD TELL THEIR KID "RESPECT THE FUCKIN TEACHER"

THERE WERE SOME PROBLEMS FOR THE TEACHERS OUTSIDE THE SCHOOL. CAR BATTERIES. TIRES AND HUBCAPS WERE TARGETS FOR SOME WHO WERE LOOKING TO GET SOME MONEY SELLING THEM. THERE'S A STORY THAT A PRINCIPAL. BOUGHT BACK HIS HUBCAPS FOR $30 WITH NO QUESTIONS ASKED. THERE WERE TIMES THAT CARS WERE VANDALIZED, BROKEN MIRRORS, BROKEN AERIALS AND FLAT TIRES. SOME NEIGHBORHOOD TOUGHS WOULD HANGOUT ON THE CORNER ACROSS THE STREET OF THE SCHOOL AT DISMISSAL LOOKING TO APPROACH THE GIRLS OR HASSLE SOME BOYS. THEY COULD BE

CHASED OFF THE SCHOOL BLOCK, BUT IT WAS NOT ILLEGAL TO BE ON THE OTHER SIDE OF THE STREET. YOU CAN SURMISE THAT THEY WERE NOT THERE TO BE HELPFUL CITIZENS. INSIDE THE SCHOOL THE STUDENTS AND TEACHERS FELT SAFE.

## *DISTRICT SUPERINTENDANT JOINS THE BUMS CLUB*

A FEW YEARS INTO THE BUMS CLUB EXISTANCE THE DISTRICT SUPERINTENDANT WITH THE REPUTATION OF A TOUGH NO NONSENSE GUY, GOT THE WORD THAT THERE'S A GROUP OF GUYS IN A TEACHERS' ROOM HAVING A GOOD TIME. HE WAS TOLD THAT THIS GROUP OF TEACHERS CALLED THEMSELVES THE BUMS. HE WANTED TO SEE WHAT THIS ROOM WAS ALL ABOUT. DURING A SCHOOL VISIT, HE OPENED THE DOOR GETTING A GLIMPSE OF A TEACHER SLEEPING ON THE COT AND A GROUP OF LOUD TEACHERS IN A MESSY ROOM. HE SAW TEACHERS LAUGHING AND ENJOYING EACH OTHER. HE SHOOK HIS HEAD AND LEFT. A FEW DAYS LATER THE DISTRICT SUPERINTENDANT REQUESTED TO BE A MEMBER OF THE BUMS CLUB.
MR. S. AUTHORED A BUMS' CLUB APPLICATION WHICH WAS SENT TO THE DISTRICT OFFICE, CARE OF MR. WILLIAM, THE SUPERINTENDANT. THE APPLICATION HAD A GROUP OF QUESTIONS. ONE QUESTION WAS YOUR HIGHEST LEVEL OF EDUCATION ONLY HAVING ELEMENTARY\_\_\_\_ OR JUNIOR HIGH SCHOOL\_\_\_\_ AS CHOICES. ANOTHER QUESTION WAS FUNNY TO THE BUMS. IF ACCEPTED, WHICH COMMITTEES WOULD YOU LIKE TO SERVE ON? THE COMMITTEES LISTED WERE THINGS FAMILIAR TO THE BUMS. THE BELL COMMITTEE, THE TIMECLOCK COMMITTEE, THE BUMS ROOM SPEAKER COMMITTEE AND A FEW MORE. THE REASONS FOR THESE COMMITTEES WAS AS FOLLOWS. WHILE WAITING FOR THE GONG TO RING AT DISMISSAL TIME, SOMEONE WOULD THROW THEIR KEYS HITTING THE GONG, CAUSING THE CLASSES ON THAT FLOOR TO BE DISMISSED A FEW MINUTES SOONER. AT PUNCHOUT TIME, TEACHERS PUT THEIR TIMECARD BEHIND A WILLING TEACHER'S CARD. THAT TEACHER WOULD PUNCH THE TIMECARD OF

MANY OTHER TEACHERS. IN THE BUMS ROOM THE SPEAKER GIVING THE MORNING ANNOUNCEMENTS WAS SOMETIMES REMOVED WITH A WINDOW POLE. TO BE SURE THE DISTRICT SUPERINTENDANT DID NOT KNOW THE MEANINGS OF THESE COMMITTEES ON HIS APPLICATION. MR. WILLIAM THE DISTRICT SUPERINTENDANT PROMPTLY AND SATISFACTORILY SUBMITTED THE APPLICATION FOR APPROVAL. MR. WILLIAM BECAME A MEMBER OF THE BUMS CLUB.

SOON AFTER, MR. MARIO, THE UNION DISTRICT REPRESENTATIVE, REQUESTED AND WAS GRANTED MEMBERSHIP IN OUR CLUB OF CHARACTERS. DID THE BUMS CLUB MEMBERS GET ANY FAVORS OR SPECIAL TREATMENT FROM THESE TWO VERY, VERY INFLUENTIAL MEMBERS, YOU DECIDE.

## BUMS GROUP 2=== *MORE TERRIFIC BUMS*

IN GROUP #2 THERE ARE SEVEN BUMS FROM YOUNG GUYS TO OLDER MILITARY VETERANS. THERE ARE TEACHERS LICENSED IN PHYSICAL EDUCATION, MATH, SCIENCE, SOCIAL STUDIES AND MAYBE MUSIC. ALTHOUGH ONE GUY WAS SENT TO JUNIOR HIGH SCHOOL 50 AS A MUSIC TEACHER, HE REFUSED TO PLAY THE PIANO OR ANY INSTRUMENT DURING HIS MUSIC CLASSES OR THE PRESENTING OF THE FLAG CEREMONY IN THE AUDITORIUM. ALL ABOUT BUMDOM!

NO FULL NAMES TO PROTECT THE GUILTY.

MR. STANLEY===BOOK CONTRIBUTOR==LIVELY COMING IN, LIVELY LEAVING THE BUMS ROOM.

MR. STANLEY, A CONTRIBUTOR TO THIS BOOK, APPLIED FOR A SIX MONTH SABATICAL. THE APPLICATION WAS TO BE ACCOMPANIED WITH THE EDUCATIONAL BENEFITS FROM THIS SABATICAL AND A REASON SUPPORTING THE REQUEST FOR THE LEAVE WITH PAY. AFTER MR. STANLEY SUBMITTED THE PAPERS, HE INQUIRED AS TO WHAT MORE HAD TO BE SUBMITTED TO THE DISTRICT OFFICE. MR. MARIO, OUR DISTRICT REP. AND GREAT BUM, TOLD HIM "JUST WRITE ANYTHING, WHO GIVES A F____". THE ISSUE EASILY RESOLVED.

MR. STANLEY WAS A VERY NIMBLE MARSHALL ARTS INSTRUCTOR. IN THE BUMS ROOM HE WAS KNOWN FOR DOING THE MONKEY WHICH MEANT JUMPING ON THE CHAIRS, TABLES AND THE WINDOWSILL. WHEN LEAVING THE BUMS ROOM HE WOULD GO OUT THE DOOR YELLING WE HAVE NOT YET BEGUN TO FIGHT OR YELLING BONSAI, BONZAI OR SOME OTHER

BATTLE CRY AS HE STARTED WALKING OUT OF THE BUMS ROOM TO TEACH A CLASS.

MR. SAM 1===SECOND APPEARANCE== OUR BORN VICTIM, IN TROUBLE WITH THE WORLD.

MR. SAM 1 GOT INTO BIG TROUBLE. A VERY PRETTY READING TEACHER WAS ASSIGNED TO JUNIOR HIGH SCHOOL 50 TWICE A WEEK. ONE MORNING MR. SAM 1 THOUGHT IT WAS NICE TO GREET HER WITH A HUG. APPARENTLY, SHE DIDN'T THINK THAT MR. SAM 1 WAS HUGGABLE AND MADE A COMPLAINT TO THE DISTRICT OFFICE. MR. SAM 1 WAS ASKED TO DEFEND HIS FRIENDLY GREETING AT THE DISTRICT OFFICE. THE DAY BEFORE THE HEARING, A PHONE CALL FROM MR. MARIO, OUR DISTRICT REP. ASKED IF MR. SAM 1 WAS A BUM. WITH THE ANSWER BEING YES, MR. MARIO ASSURED ME THAT THERE WOULD BE NO CONSEQUENCES FOR MR. SAM 1. WHEN MR. SAM 1 RETURNED TO JUNIOR HIGH SCHOOL 50, HE SAID THAT HE WAS REALLY ADMONISHED AT THE MEETING BUT NOTHING MORE. THAT DAY MR. MARIO TOLD ME THAT HE WANTED TO ASK THE READING TEACHER TO SPEND THE NIGHT WITH HIM.

MR. BEN 1===BIG GUY==BOOMING VOICE==SAID IT THE WAY IT WAS==EVERYDAY WAS DRESS DOWN DAY.

SOMETIMES THINGS ARE SAID IN A SPECIAL WAY. A DAY AFTER THE REPORT CARDS WERE DISTRIBUTED, AN UNPLEASANT STUDENT CAME TO SCHOOL AND REQUESTED HIS REPORT CARD. MR. BEN 1 LOOKED AT THE BOY AND SAID, "SORRY SON I WIPED MY ASS WITH IT".

ONE DAY WHEN MR. BEN 1 ENTERED THE MAIN OFFICE A SECRETARY CHIDED HIM FOR HIS MODE OF DRESS. A COUPLE WORDS WERE SAID THAT CAUSED MR. BEN 1 TO TURNOVER THE SECRETARY'S DESK. WHEN HE WAS SUMMONED TO THE DISTRICT OFFICE, HE WAS TOLD THAT IT'S NOT THE BEST THING TO DO, TRY NOT TO DO IT AGAIN.

THE ASSISTANT PRINCIPAL WHO WAS THE OBJECT OF THE CAUGHT IN THE VICE RAID HEADLINE PRANK WAS TALKING TO MR. BEN 1 NEAR THE BUMS ROOM. WHILE THEY WERE TALKING HE DECIDED TO PICK HER UP AND CARRY HER OVER HIS SHOULDER, SLAPPING HER ON HER BACKSIDE WHILE GOING UP THE FLIGHT OF STEPS. LET ME ADD, FOR WHATEVER HER REASON NO COMPLAINTS WERE MADE. MR. S. CLAIMED, ACCORDING TO SOME PRIMITIVE CULTURES THEY WOULD BE OBLIGATED TO BE MARRIED.

MR. JERRY===PRANKIST==BUMS ROOM PROVOKER==LOOKS FOR FUNNEEE ==AUTHOR OF "THE BUMS CLUB"

MR. JERRY===ALSO HAD A GUIDANCE COUNSELOR LICENSE AND AFTER 25 YEARS IN THE CLASSROOM HE REQUESTED A GUIDANCE POSITION. MR. MARIO TOOK CARE OF PLACING MR. JERRY AT JUNIOR HIGH SCHOOL 50 AS A GUIDANCE COUNSELOR. A FEW YEARS LATER, MR. MARIO NOMINATED MR. JERRY TO REPRESENT THE DISTRICT AT THE BOARD OF EDUCATION FOR THE COUNSELOR RECOGNITION CEREMONY. A BUM HELPING ANOTHER BUM. THE PLAQUE SHOULD HAVE BEEN HUNG ON THE BATHROOM DOOR IN THE BUMS ROOM.

Counselor Recognition Plaque

MR. JERRY WAS ONCE THE MATH CHAIRMAN. HE HAD A KEY TO A SUPPLY ROOM. MRS. GOLDIE MADE A COMPLAINT TO HIM ABOUT NOT GETTING ANY GRAPH PAPER. A COUPLE OF BUMS GOT INVOLVED WITH THIS VERY NICE MATH TEACHER. MR. JERRY AND MR.

VINNY TOLD HER TO WRITE A RED B, STANDING FOR BUMS MEMBER, ON THE TOP CORNER OF THE SUPPLY REQUEST FORM. WHEN WE WERE TOLD THAT SHE SUBMITTED THE FORM WITH THE RED B, MR. JERRY AND MR. VINNY HAD MONITORS BRING A LOAD OF SUPPLIES TO MRS. GOLDIE. SHE GOT WASTEPAPER BASKETS, OLD MATH TEXTBOOKS, CHALK, OLD DISCOLORED PAPER AND STUFF, BUT NO GRAPH PAPER. SHE COMPLAINED TO THE MONITORS WITH EACH SHIPMENT, I DON'T NEED OLD BOOKS, I NEED GRAPH PAPER. THE NEXT DAY THERE WAS GRAPH PAPER IN HER MAILBOX.

MR. DICK===NOT OPERATING AT FULL SPEED==COMES WITH SHOPPING WAGON WITH MANY BOOKS IN IT==APPOINTED TO JUNIOR HIGH SCHOOL 50 AS A MUSIC TEACHER==HE REFUSED TO PLAY ANY MUSIC, EVEN WHEN ASKED BY THE SUPERVISOR.

WHEN HE ASKED TO BE IN THE BUMS CLUB, MR. JOHN TOLD HIM THAT THERE WOULD BE AN INITIATION. MR. DICK AGREED TO THE TIE BURNING CEREMONY. THE IDEA BEING SINCE HE DOESN'T SEE MANY GUYS WEARING TIES, HE SHOULD BE ONE OF THE BOYS AND GET RID OF HIS TIE. THERE WAS A SMALL GROUP IN THE BUMS ROOM WHEN MR. JOHN STARTED THE CEREMONY BY CUTTING OFF MR. DICK'S TIE NEAR THE KNOT. THIS WAS QUITE A SIGHT.
NOBODY IN THE ROOM HAD MATCHES SO THE PRINCIPAL WHO SMOKED WAS ASKED TO COME INTO THE BUMS ROOM. PRINCIPAL FRANK PROVIDED THE MATCHES AND THE TIE BURNING CEREMONY CONTINUED. THE TIE WAS FIRED UP. IT FLAMED UP QUICKLY CAUSING MR. JOHN TO DROP IT ON THE TABLE WHICH STARTED BURNING. THE PRINCIPAL RAN OUT OF THE ROOM REPEATING I WASN'T HERE, I

WASN'T HERE. THE TIE WAS GONE, THE FIRE WAS EXTINGUISHED AND MR. DICK WAS A BUM BY A UNANIMOUS VOTE.

MR. DICK WOULD ENTER AND LEAVE THE SCHOOL WITH HIS SHOPPING WAGON PACKED WITH BOOKS. IT SEEMED THAT HE DIDN'T USE THE BOOKS, READ THE BOOKS OR KNOW WHICH BOOKS WERE IN THE WAGON. WHEN ASSISTANT PRINCIPAL BERNIE ASKED HIM TO PLAY IN THE AUDITORIUM, HE SAID, NO! HE WOULD JUST SIT AT THE PIANO.

MR. JOHN===PRANKPRO==MORNING WORKOUTS IN THE SCHOOL GYM== ARTIST==GEOLOGIST==HIGHLY THOUGHT OF IN THE WORLD OF BUMDOM.

MR. DICK CAME TO JUNIOR HIGH SCHOOL 50 WITH A SHOPPING WAGON BUT WOULD NOT TELL US THE NAMES OF ANY OF THE BOOKS IN THE WAGON. AS YOU ENTER THE SCHOOL THROUGH THE MAIN ENTRANCE THERE'S A LARGE DISPLAY CASE. IT IS MAINLY FOR TROPHIES AND AWARDS. MR. JOHN AND MR. VINNY GOT THE KEY AND SUCCESSFULLY DISPLAYED THE MR. DICK SHOPPING WAGON FOR ALL TO SEE IN THE MAIN LOBBY DISPLAY WINDOW. AT DISMISSAL MR. DICK WAS LOOKING FOR HIS SHOPPING WAGON. HE EVENTUALLY SAW IT OUTRAGIOULY VISIBLE IN THE MAIN LOBBY DISPLAY WINDOW. WHOEVER SAW IT WONDERED WHAT IT WAS DOING THERE. THIS OUT OF SHAPE PRANK CAUSED MANY SMILES WHEN PEOPLE SAW THE SHOPPING CART IN THE MAIN LOBBY DISPLAY CASE.

MR. AL 3===VOICE OF DOOM==NOTHING IS GOOD==ALL BAD== ALWAYS GREAT TO HAVE HIM PRESENT IN THE BUMS ROOM.

MR. AL 3 SITS AT A TABLE NEAR THE WINDOW CONTINUOSLY DRUMMING ON THE TABLE WITH HIS TWO FISTS. OTHER TIMES HE PLAYS MUSIC BLOWING HIS COMB WRAPPED IN TOILET PAPER. HE LIKES TO SIT IN THAT CORNER WAITING TO INTERJECT SOMETHING THAT WILL UPSET SOMEONE.

A TEACHER AND HIS WIFE WORKED AT JUNIOR HJGH SCHOOL 50 WHEN THEY WERE HAVING A HOUSE BUILT IN A DEVELOPMENT IN QUEENS NEW YORK. THE CONSTRUCTION STOPPED BECAUSE THE CONTRACTOR RAN OUT OF MONEY. WHEN THE TEACHER CAME INTO THE BUMS ROOM, MR. AL 3 STARTED HIS TIRADE SAYING, YOU WILL NEVER GET INTO THAT HOUSE. YOU WILL NEVER SEE YOUR MONEY BACK. `THE OUTCOME FOR THE TEACHER WAS EACH PURCHASER HAD TO PAY A FEW THOUSAND DOLLARS MORE AND THE HOUSES WERE COMPLETED. ONE DAY, THE WIFE CAME INTO THE BUMS ROOM AND INVITED ALL OF THE BUMS TO A BARBEQUE AT THEIR NEW HOUSE. WITH THIS, SHE LOOKED AT MR. AL 3 SAYING, NOT YOU, NOT YOU!!

## NEIGHBORHOOD STORES

WHEN A TEACHER IS NOT ASSIGNED TO A CLASS FOR TWO OR MORE CONSECUTIVE PERIODS, GOING OUT TO A NEIGHBORHOOD STORE IS A NICE BREAK. WITHIN A FEW BLOCKS OF THE SCHOOL THERE WAS A VARIETY OF PLACES FOR TEACHERS TO PATRONIZE. IN ADDITION TO MOM=POP STORES, THERE WERE WELL KNOWN BRAND FACTORIES AND FOOD DISTRIBUTORS IN THE AREA.

THERE WERE A NUMBER OF HALF DAYS WHEN THE STUDENTS WENT HOME AT 12PM. DURING THESE HALF DAYS, TEACHERS HAD OBLIGATIONS LIKE FILLING OUT REPORT CARDS, ENTERING GRADES, KEEPING PUPIL RECORDS UP TO DATE, MARKING MIDTERM TESTS OR STANDARDIZED TESTS, CONFERENCES, PROCEDURE MEETINGS ETC. WHEN TEACHERS HAD THE HOUR OR MORE BREAK IT WAS A TREAT TO GETOUT TO A STORE IN THE AREA.

A FAVORITE EATERY WAS THE PASTRAMI KING WHERE MR. MARV ORDERED THE SANDWICH AND HOT CHERRY PEPPERS FOR THE BUMS ROOM HOT PEPPER EATING EVENT. THE PASTRAMI KING WAS A NEIGHBORHOOD INSTITUTION ONE BLOCK FROM THE SCHOOL UNTIL IT WAS THRASHED DURING THE NEW YORK CITY 7/13/77 BLACKOUT. THE RESTAURANT WAS WRECKED AND ROBBED BY NEIGHBORHOOD PEOPLE.
ONE BLOCK FROM JUNIOR HIGH SCHOOL 50 THERE WAS A HARDWARE STORE PATRONIZED BY TEACHERS FOR SMALL ITEMS. ONE DAY A MESSAGE WAS DELIVERED TO A TEACHER IN THE BUMS ROOM. THE TEACHER ASKED US, WHERE HE COULD GET SAKRETE. HE WAS TOLD ABOUT THE HARDWARE STORE ABOUT ONE BLOCK AWAY. THE NEXT DAY HE

CAME INTO THE BUMS ROOM SAYING HE HAD TO RETURN THE SAKRETE, HIS WIFE TOLD THE SECRETARY SHE NEEDED SACCARIN.

MR. JERRY WAS WITH MR. STANLEY AND BOSS GENE AT THE HARDWARE STORE. MR. JERRY BOUGHT A COUPLE OF THINGS TOTALLING $11.18. MR. JERRY GAVE THE OWNER THE $11 AND PUT HIS HAND IN HIS POCKET FOR THE CHANGE, BUT THE OWNER SAID FORGET ABOUT IT. WHEN WALKING BACK TO THE SCHOOL MR. STANLEY ASKED IF THE OWNER SAID FORGET ABOUT PAYING. BOSS GENE AND MR. JERRY SAID YES, HE LIKES TEACHERS. A FEW DAYS LATER, MR. STANLEY WENT TO THE HARDWARE STORE. HE CAME BACK TO THE BUMS ROOM WONDERING WHY HE PAID FULL PRICE. HE THOUGHT HE'D GET A TEACHER DISCOUNT. HE BELIEVED THE TWO PRANKSTERS. THE PRANKSTERS WOULD BE A GREAT IDEA FOR A TELEVISION SHOW.

AL A. AND EDDIE A., TWO FORMER STUDENTS OF JUNIOR HIGH SCHOOL 50 OWNED AN AUTO PARTS STORE IN THE NEIGHBORHOOD. WHEN TEACHERS WALKED INTO THEIR STORE, THEY BOTH LIT UP, HAPPY TO SEE THEIR FORMER TEACHERS. THE TEACHERS GOT A GREAT DEAL AND WONDERFUL SERVICE. MR. JERRY NEEDED MECHANICAL HELP NEAR THE SCHOOL. DEAN SAM WAS THERE TO SAVE THE DAY. HE SAW THE PROBLEM, ORDERED THE ALTINATOR FROM AL A. AND FIXED THE CAR BEFORE AFTERNOON DISMISSAL.
WE HAD WONDERFUL FOOD SUPPLIERS LIKE ACORN PRODUCTS, VITA HERRING, A CHEESECAKE BAKERY, CAKES FOR PASSOVER, DIFFERENT KINDS OF BREAD, A KOSHER SALAMI AND BOLOGNA PRODUCER AND FRIENDLY BODEGAS. ACORN'S PRETZEL RODS WERE GREAT. I DON'T KNOW IF IT WAS ABOUT PITY OR

RESPECT, BUT WE GOT SPECIAL TREATMENT FROM THE VENDORS. FRIDAY AFTERNOON THE TEACHERS FLEW TO THE CHEESECAKE PLACE TO BUY THE DAMAGED 16 SLICE CAKES. WE WERE TOLD THAT OUR PRICE WAS LESS THAN THE COST OF THE INGREDIENTS TO MAKE THE CHEESECAKES.
THE OWNER OF ACORN PRODUCTS GREW UP IN THE NEIGHBORHOOD AND WAS A FORMER STUDENT OF JUNIOR HIGH SCHOOL 50. HE LOVED TALKING WITH THE TEACHERS. WHEN MANY TEACHERS NEEDED CANDY OR THOSE LONG PRETZEL RODS FOR PARTIES, JASON AT ACORN WAS THE PLACE TO GO.
SOL AND NICKS WAS A JEWISH STYLE CORNBEEF AND PASTRAMI DELI ON SOUTH $3^{RD}$ STREET, ONE BLOCK AWAY FROM THE SCHOOL. NICK WAS ALWAYS HAPPY TO HELP TEACHERS. HE'D THROW PLENTY OF SAUERKRAUT ON THE FRANKS.

ON THE JOHN D. WELLS JUNIOR HIGH SCHOOL 50 FACEBOOK GROUP SITE, STUDENT ROBERT REMEMBERS HIS PROM AT THE POLONAISE TERRACE. THIS CATERING HALL, A COUPLE OF MILES AWAY FROM JUNIOR HIGH SCHOOL 50, WAS KNOWN FOR MORE EXTRAVAGANT OCCASIONS. MY SINGING GROUP, THE CATALINAS, PERFORMED A SIX SONG SET FOR A WEDDING AT THE POLONAISE. THE PROM WAS LAVISH WITH GIRLS IN GOWNS, BOYS IN TUXEDOS AND SOME STUDENTS HIRED LIMOUSINE SERVICE. THIS PROM EVOKED TWO DIFFERENT THOUGHTS. SOME COMMENTED THAT MANY OF THESE KIDS WERE WAY DOWN IN THEIR READING AND MATH SCORES, WHY HAVE SUCH AN EXTRAVAGANT GRADUATION PARTY? THE OPPOSITE VIEW SAID, THIS MIGHT BE THE ONLY GRADUATION PROM FOR MANY OF THESE KIDS. THEY WILL HAVE THIS WONDERFUL MEMORY FOR THE REST OF THEIR LIFE.

WITH REMEMBERING HIS PROM ROBERT ALSO WROTE, HE MISSES HIS SCHOOL FRIENDS, ENJOYED HIS CHILDHOOD. HE BECAME A CHEF AND AFTER THE PROM NEVER SAW HIS SCHOOLMATES AGAIN. THIS BOOK IS LOADED WITH LASTING MEMORIES OF JUNIOR HIGH SCHOOL 50 AND THEIR TEACHERS.

## BUMS GROUP 3===*SOME MORE BUMS*

IN GROUP 3 THERE'S FUN POKED AT A COUPLE OF GUYS, HUMOR FROM SOME OF THE GUYS, AND SOME CREATIVITY. MR. SAM 1 MAKES HIS THIRD APPEARANCE. WHEN MR. SAM 1 WAS IN THE BUMS ROOM HE USUALLY GOT PLENTY OF ATTENTION. GROUP 3 SHOULD BE FUN.

NO FULL NAMES TO PROTECT THE GUILTY.

MR. PETE 1===GYM TEACHER==USUALLY SITS ON THE BACK OF THE CHAIR, FEET ON THE SEAT==FUN TALKER==DOESN'T GIVE A SHIT ATTITUDE==HORSE RACING PICKS IN THE MORNING==BUMS ROOM CONTRIBUTOR

MR. PETE 1 HAD THE G.O. COORDINATOR POSITION. I THINK G.O, STOOD FOR GENERAL ORGANIZATION. ABOUT HALF THE TEACHERS ARE ASSIGNED A HOMEROOM WHILE THE OTHERS HAVE A DIFFERENT SCHOOL RELATED RESPONSIBILITY. AS G.O. COORDINATOR, MR. PETE 1 ACCEPTED THE IDEA OF BIG BUTTONS FOR THE GRADUATING CLASS. THAT FALL HE ORDERED THE BUTTONS TO BE DISTRIBUTED TO THE SENIORS IN THE SPRING BEFORE GRADUATION. HE ORDERED 450 BUTTONS FOR THE GRADUATING CLASS OF 1987. WHEN HE ORDERED THEM IN THE FALL IT WAS 1987, BUT WHEN THEY GRADUATED NEXT JUNE IT WAS 1988. THIS TIME MR. PETE 1 WAS AHEAD OF SCHEDULE.

IF A STUDENT PAID THE G.O. DUES, THE STUDENT WAS ENTITLED TO ATTEND THE SHOWING OF A G.O. MOVIE. AT MOVIE TIME THE AUDITORIUM WAS FULL OF PAID STUDENTS. THE AUDIO=VISUAL SQUAD PUT THE LAST REEL ON FIRST AND THE FIRST REEL WAS

SHOWN LAST. SOME KIDS THOUGHT THEY SAW TWO MOVIES.
MR. PETE 1 LIKED PICKING HORSES AND GETTING OUT A LITTLE EARLY TO BE AT THE TRACK. HE LIKED LOOKING AT THE RACING PAGES IN THE BUMS ROOM. HE SAW A COUPLE OF SURE BETS AND THOUGHT HE HAD AN OPPORTUNITY TO LEAVE SCHOOL EARLY AND GET TO THE TRACK. AS HE WAS LEAVING THE BUILDING, ASSISTANT PRINCIPAL JERRY CASUALLY ASKED WHERE ARE YOU HEADING? MR. PETE 1 SAID TO THE POST OFFICE. ASSISTANT PRINCIPAL JERRY SAID, ME TOO. MR. PETE 1 BOUGHT A BOOK OF STAMPS AND CAME BACK TO THE SCHOOL.

MR. SAM 1===THIRD APPEARANCE==HE COULD BE FUNNY.

MR. SAM 1===REMEMBER HIS HUGGING MISHAP, THE COVERAGE PRANK AND THE DENTIST PULLING THE WRONG TOOTH.
MR. SAM 1 ACTUALLY DID HAVE HAD A SENSE OF HUMOR. THERE WAS ONE DOOR TO HIS CLASSROOM, HE PLACED A SIGN ON THE DOOR SAYING PLEASE USE OTHER DOOR.
ONE YEAR THE BOARD OF EDUCATION THOUGHT IT WOULD BE BENEFICIAL FOR THE CHILDREN TO HAVE THEIR EYESIGHT CHECKED BY A CLASSROOM TEACHER. THERE WAS AN EYE CHART, KIDS COVERING EACH EYE, THEN READING TO THE LOWEST LINE. MR. SAM 1 HAD HIS OWN METHOD OF TESTING AND WRITING THE RESULTS. IF THE STUDENT DID NOT WEAR GLASSES, MR. SAM 1 WROTE 20/20, IF THE KID WORE GLASSES MR. SAM 1 WROTE 40/40.

MR. BEN 2===INTELLECTUAL==SPOKE MANY LANGUAGES—HUMOROUS==COLLEGE PROFESSOR TYPE==ALWAYS WITH SPORT JACKET AND TIE.

THERE WAS QUIET IN MOST CLASSES, BUT IN SOME CLASSES THE NOISE WAS OVERWHELMING. MR. BEN 2 HAD A HIGH VOLUMED CLASS. HE DID NOT PUT FORTH BIG ENERGY TO KEEP THE VOLUME DOWN. ONE DAY MR. BEN 2 ENTERED THE BUMS ROOM AFTER A NOISY CLASS SAYING, THERE'S ONE GOOD THING ABOUT A NOISY CLASS, "YOU CAN FART AND NOBODY HEARS IT!". WITH THIS HE PICKED UP HIS NEW YORK TIMES AND WAITED TO GO TO HIS NEXT CLASS SO HE CAN F=== AGAIN, PEACEFULLY.

MR. ARTIE 1===PLAYED ACCORDIAN AT THE TEACHER TALENT SHOW==HAD A SPECIAL NEEDS CLASS==A CREATIVE TEACHER

A STAFF MEMBER COULD MAKE AN APPOINTMENT TO GET A SHOESHINE IN HIS CLASSROOM. MR. ARTIE 1 BOUGHT SHOESHINE BOXES COMPLETELY EQUIPED FOR STUDENTS THAT WANTED ONE. THE THOUGHT WAS THERE ARE MANY LESSONS THAT CAN BE LEARNED HAVING A SHOESHINE BOX. MATH, READING, BUSINESS AND SOCIAL SKILLS CAN BE DEVELOPED WITH A SHOESHINE SERVICE. SOME TEACHERS WERE PLEASED TO PATRONIZE THE STUDENTS AND IN TURN WALK AROUND WITH NICE SHINY SHOES. THESE KIDS WERE ABLE TO GO TO THE BODEGA ACROSS THE STREET FROM THE SCHOOL WITH MONEY THAT THEY EARNED.

MR. ROBERT 1===QUITE FIT==MARSHALL ARTS INSTRUCTOR==EASY GOING—EVERYTHING IS GREAT ATTITUDE

HE HAD AN INTERESTING PHILOSOPHY AT WORK. COMPLAIN AS SOON AS YOUR SUPERVISOR APPROACHES YOU. COMPLAIN ABOUT SOMETHING THAT THEY CAN SOLVE AND THEY WILL THINK TWICE BEFORE THEY BOTHER YOU.

IN A BUILDING WHERE HE TAUGHT KARATE, HE NOTICED A FLYER ASKING FOR PEOPLE INTERESTED IN TEACHING A MEMORY IMPROVEMENT COURSE. THIS WAS THE COURSE SPONSORED BY THE GUY THAT WROTE THE BOOK. MR. ROBERT 1 WAS HIRED, GIVEN THE TRAINING AND THE NECESSARY MATERIALS FOR THE COURSE. MR. ROBERT 1 DID NOT REMEMBER TO SHOW UP FOR THE FIRST SESSION. AFTER SHOWING UP FOR THE NEXT FEW SESSIONS, HE TOLD US HE QUIT. HE KNEW HE WOULD NEVER REMEMBER THE STUDENTS' NAMES.

MR. MARK===A SENIOR TEACHER== ATTENDED ALL BUMS CLUB EVENTS==HE WAS THE BUMS CLUB LABORATORY TECHNICIAN.

MR. STANLEY WAS SO HAPPY THAT HE DIDN'T HAVE TO SPEND TIME GOING TO A LAB BECAUSE MR. MARK WAS ABLE TO COLLECT HIS BLOOD RIGHT IN THE BUMS ROOM. MR. MARK PROVIDED A SERVICE NOT DONE IN ANY OTHER TEACHERS' LOUNGE. THIS WAS ONLY DONE IN THE BUMS ROOM OF JUNIOR HIGH SCHOOL 50.
MR. MARK WAS THE GUY SLEEPING ON THE OLD, SUNKEN IN COT WHEN DISTRICT SUPERINTENDANT WILLIAM LOOKED INTO THE BUMS ROOM AND APPLIED FOR BUMS CLUB MEMBERSHIP.

MR. NEFTI===LIKED THE BUMS ROOM, OFTEN SMILING AT THE CONVERSATIONS==LIKED WALKING

FOR FRESH RYE BREADS AND CHALLAH IN TWO NEIGHBORHOOD BAKERIES PATRONIZED BY US BUMS.

ALTHOUGH MR. NEFTI WAS ABLE TO AVOID TROUBLE AS A TEACHER AT JUNIOR HIGH SCHOOL 50, HE WENT OUT OF CONTROL WHEN HE BECAME THE PRINCIPAL OF ANOTHER SCHOOL. HE MADE THE FRONT PAGE OF A MAJOR NEWSPAPER. HIS PICTURE WITH HIS PROTECTIVE VEST AND HIS BOMB THE SCHOOL STATEMENT WAS ON THE FRONT PAGE OF THE DAILY NEWS. THIS ACTION CAUSED QUITE A STIR AT THAT NEIGHBORHOOD SCHOOL. WE KNEW HIS BUMS QUALITIES WOULD BE UNCOVERED. HERE THEY REALLY EXPLODED. HIS DEMOTION, BEING REINSTATED, FRONT PAGE PICTURE AND ALL THE REST WAS PROBABLY INFLUENCED BY HANGING OUT IN THE BUMS ROOM OF JUNIOR HIGH SCHOOL 50.

## *HOMEROOM AND QUOTA TEACHERS*

USUALLY, THE SCHOOL HAD ABOUT TWICE AS MANY STAFF MEMBERS AS CLASSES. EACH CLASS HAD ONE "HOMEROOM" TEACHER ASSIGNED TO IT. HOMEROOM TEACHER MEANT A RESPONSIBILITY TO BE IN THE ROOM TO TAKE THE MORNING ATTENDANCE AND TO BE IN THE ROOM AT DISMISSAL TIME. IN ADDITION, HOMEROOM TEACHERS HAD VARIOUS CLERICAL CHORES. THINGS LIKE KEEPING PUPIL RECORDS UP TO DATE, FILLING OUT REPORT CARDS, TAKING DAILY ATTENDANCE, DISTRIBUTING NOTICES ETC.

"QUOTA" TEACHERS HAD VARIOUS SCHOOL RELATED JOBS. THERE WERE LUNCHROOM DUTIES, GRADE ADVISORS, YEARBOOK, LIBRARY, SENIOR ACTIVITIES, CHORUS, BAND, MORNING COVERAGES, UNION REPRESENTATIVE, SCHOOL ACCOUNTS, SCIENCE LAB, DEAN, AUDIO VISUAL COORDINATOR, ATTENDANCE IMPROVEMENT DROPOUT PREVENTION FACILITATOR, SUBJECT CHAIRMAN, G.O. COORDINATOR AND OTHER POSSIBILTIES. QUOTA TEACHERS HAD NO HOMEROOM AND MIGHT HAVE LESS TEACHING PERIODS. WHEN A QUOTA POSITION WAS POSTED, TEACHERS WOULD APPLY LOOKING FOR A CHANCE TO GET AWAY FROM THE HOMEROOM AND HAVE LESS TEACHING PERIODS. IF THE PRINCIPAL AVOIDS THE TEACHER CONTRACT BY ASSIGNING THE POSITION WITHOUT POSTING THE POSITION, TEACHERS CAN SUBMIT A GRIEVANCE WHICH MIGHT HAVE TO BE ARBITRATED. MR. STANLEY WENT TO ARBITRATION AND WON TO GET THE ATTENDANCE IMPROVEMENT DROPOUT PREVENTION FACILITATOR POSITION.

## *ATTENDANCE IMPROVEMENT DROPOUT PREVENTION PROGRAM*

A.I.D.P. WAS A PROGRAM SETUP TO REDUCE EXCESSIVE ABSENCE. ANY STUDENT ABSENT 50 OR MORE DAYS DURING THE PREVIOUS SCHOOL YEAR WAS PLACED IN THE ATTENDANCE IMPROVEMENT DROPOUT PREVENTION PROGRAM. THE PARENTS WERE NOTIFIED OF THE REASONS, THE GOALS AND THE PROCEDURES OF THE PROGRAM. A TEACHER, GIVEN THE TITLE FACILITATOR, WAS IN CHARGE OF THE DAILY CONTACTS AND MEETINGS. THE TEACHER HAD A TEAM OF A GUIDANCE COUNSELOR, A MALE AIDE AND A FEMALE AIDE TO MAKE HOME VISITS. BECAUSE OF THE POSSIBILITIES OF A HOME VISIT AND CHILD ABUSE CHARGES FOR NOT HAVING THE CHILD IN SCHOOL, PARENTS MADE THE EXTRA EFFORT TO HAVE THEIR CHILD ATTEND SCHOOL.

THE FEW YEARS THAT THE ATTENDANCE IMPROVEMENT DROPOUT PREVENTION PROGRAM EXISTED AT JUNIOR HIGH SCHOOL 50 EVERY FACILITATOR OF THE PROGRAM WAS A BUM. TEACHERS WERE PLACED ACCORDING TO SENIORITY. THE BUMS CLUB WAS IN EXISTANCE MORE THAN TWENTY YEARS, THEREFORE MANY BUMS HAD SENIORITY. A.I.D.P. WAS A NICE CHANGE FROM HAVING A HOMEROOM AND A FULL TEACHING PROGRAM.
WHEN A STUDENT WAS ABSENT THE PARENT WAS NOTIFIED. AFTER A STUDENT WAS OUT FROM SCHOOL THREE CONSECUTIVE DAYS THERE COULD BE A HOME VISIT BY AN AIDE. THE FULL PROGRAM WAS MONITORED BY A SUPERVISOR FROM THE BOARD OF EDUCATION AND DEAN SAM WHO BECAME OUR DISTRICT SUPERVISOR.

ONE MORNING THERE WAS A DISTRICT WIDE ATTENDANCE IMPROVEMENT DROPOUT PREVENTION MEETING AT THE DISTRICT 14 OFFICE. MR. STANLEY THE JUNIOR HIGH SCHOOL 50 FACILITATOR AND MR. JERRY THE GUIDANCE COUNSELOR OF THE PROGRAM WALKED TO THE MEETING. AT THE END OF THE MEETING, DEAN SAM OFFERED US A RIDE BACK TO JUNIOR HIGH SCHOOL 50 IN HIS BEAUTIFUL CADILLAC. MR. STANLEY AND MR. JERRY SAT IN THE BACK SEAT OF THIS NICE CADILLAC. DEAN SAM AND A BOARD OF EDUCATION REPRESENTATIVE WERE IN THE FRONT SEATS. THE REPRESENTATIVE COMMENTED ABOUT THE BEAUTIFUL CADILLAC ON THE RIDE BACK TO JUNIOR HIGH SCHOOL 50. MR. JERRY BLURTED OUT AND ALSO WITH A BLACK CHAUFFEUR. THE BOARD OF EDUCATION REP. DID NOT KNOW WHAT TO SAY.

ONE MORNING THE ATTENDANCE IMPROVEMENT DROPOUT PREVENTION PROGRAM WAS TO BE MONITORED BY SOMEONE FROM THE BOARD OF EDUCATION. A VERY ATTRACTIVE WOMAN CAME TO JUNIOR HIGH SCHOOL 50 ACCOMPANIED BY OUR DEAN SAM, OUR A.I.D.P. DISTRICT SUPERVISOR AND IMPRESSIVE CADILLAC OWNER. OUR PROGRAM SUPPLIED ITS STUDENTS WITH MONOGRAMED BACKPACKS, HATS AND SHIRTS. THE YOUNG DAUGHTER OF THE MONITOR NOW WAS GIVEN A NICE BACKPACK, HAT AND SHIRT. THE QUESTIONS WERE VERY FEW AND WE NEVER SAW HER AGAIN. BUT WE UNDERSTAND THAT DEAN SAM DID SEE HER AGAIN. THAT YEAR THE SCHOOL ATTENDANCE NUMBERS JUMPED OVER THE ELIGIBILITY NUMBERS FOR THE PROGRAM. THE ATTENDANCE IMPROVEMENT DROPOUT PREVENTION PROGRAM WAS ELIMINATED FROM JUNIOR HIGH SCHOOL 50.

MR. JERRY WAS QUOTED IN THE SUNDAY NEW YORK TIMES EDUCATION SECTION, SPEAKING ABOUT THE POSITIVE AFFECTS OF THE PROGRAM. HAVING STUDENTS AND PARENTS VISIT THEIR ZONED HIGH SCHOOL TO GET ACQUAINTED WITH THE PHYSICAL FACILITY AND PERSONNEL BEFORE THE START OF THE NEXT SCHOOL YEAR WAS QUITE BENEFICIAL. IT GAVE THE STUDENTS THE FEELING THAT THEY WERE NOW HIGH SCHOOL STUDENTS.

## BUMS GROUP 4===*THE BUMS KEEP COMING*

IN GROUP 4 THREE NEW BUMS ARE INTRODUCED, THE OTHER FOUR ARE REPEATERS WITH INTERESTING STORIES. IN THIS GROUP THERE'S THE ONLY ADMINISTRATOR THAT ATTENDED THE FIRST BUMS BASH. ALSO, THE DISTRICT SUPERINTENDANT WHO FILLED OUT THE RIDICULOUS APPLICATION TO BE A BUMS CLUB MEMBER. TWO REPEATERS ARE THE PRANKERER WHO WAS CALLED THE TRIP KING AND OUR PRANKPRO, WHO DISPLAYED THE NEW MUSIC TEACHER'S SHOPPING WAGON IN THE MAIN ENTRANCE SHOWCASE. THIS IS A CREW WORTHY OF BUMDOM.

NO FULL NAMES TO PROTECT THE GUILTY.

ASSISSTANT PRINCIPAL BERNIE=== ==SUPPORTS TEACHERS==ATTENDED THE FIRST BUMS BASH INSTEAD OF A SUPERVISORS GATHERING.

IF A STUDENT WAS SENT TO HIS OFFICE BECAUSE OF POOR CLASS BEHAVIOR, ASSISSTANT PRINCIPAL BERNIE WAS KNOWN FOR HIS STUDENT NOSE AND TOES POSITION. HE WOULD ASK THE STUDENT TO STAND AGAINST THE WALL WITH THE NOSE AND THE TOES TOUCHING THE WALL AT THE SAME TIME. THIS METHOD MAY NOT BE ALLOWED TODAY AS WELL AS MANY OTHER DISCIPINE METHODS OF THE PAST. PUTTING A KID IN THE CORNER OR HAVING A STUDENT WRITE 100 TIMES I MUST NOT TOUCH ANOTHER STUDENT ARE CONDEMNED BY MANY IN THE EDUCATION FIELD. WHAT DO YOU THINK ABOUT NOSE AND TOES?

ONE DAY THERE WAS A LESSON ABOUT THE USE OF THE DECIMAL. ASSISTANT PRINCIPAL BERNIE CAME

INTO THE CLASSROOM. THE LESSON WAS EXPLAINED AND WRITTEN ON THE BOARD. THERE WAS A WARMUP TO SHOW THE USE OF THE DECIMAL POINT. ASSISTANT PRINCIPAL BERNIE CAME INTO THE ROOM, SAW THE TOPIC OF THE DAY AND TOOK THE CHALK. HE WROTE HIS DECIMAL ON THE BOARD AND ASKED THE CLASS 'WHAT IS THIS CALLED?" A KID YELLED OUT A DOT. ASSISTANT PRINCIPAL BERNIE MADE IT BIGGER. A KID YELLED OUT A DIME. THE ASSISTANT PRINCIPAL POINTED TO THE LESSON, MADE IT BIGGER AND A KID YELLED OUT A NICKEL. ASSISTANT PRINCIPAL BERNIE GAVE THE CHALK BACK TO THE TEACHER AND WENT BACK TO HIS OFFICE.

MR. WARREN===PRANKERER==SECOND APPEARANCE==NAMED MR. DICK, THE WHITE SHADOW==HUNG THE ASSISTANT PRINCIPAL MISS AUDREY CAUGHT IN THE VICE RAID HEADLINE OVER THE BUMS ROOM DOOR.

ASSISTANT PRINCIPAL AUDREY PROPOSED HAVING AN ARISTA PROGRAM AT JUNIOR HIGH SCHOOL 50. SHE SPOKE ABOUT ARISTA PINS, A CEREMONY, PARENT INVOLVEMENT, ALL OF IT. MR. WARREN AND HIS COHORTS SOMEHOW WERE ABLE TO HAVE SOME OF THE WORST PUPILS RECEIVE A 90+ AVERAGE AND ATTEND THE ARISTA MEETING. IT WAS A SITE TO SEE, THE WORST KIDS SEATED AT THE ARISTA MEETING WITH THE BEST STUDENTS IN THE SCHOOL. AN ARISTA PROGRAM DIDN'T COME TO PASS BUT JUNIOR HIGH SCHOOL 50 DID HAVE AN HONOR ROLL WITHOUT THE MR. WARREN NOMINEES.

A SHOP TEACHER WAS QUITE ROTUND. LARGE AROUND THE MIDSECTION. SO LARGE THAT MR.

WARREN NAMED HIS BELT THE BELT PARKWAY, WHICH IS A ROAD AROUND BROOKLYN, NY.

MR. JOHN===PRANKPRO==SECOND APPEARANCE==HE DID THE TIE CUTTING, TIE BURNING CEREMONY==HE PUT THE MR. DICK SHOPPING WAGON IN THE SCHOOL DISPLAY CASE ==A GREAT BUMS ROOM CONTRIBUTOR.

MR. JOHN BECAME A LICENSED STOCKBROKER. HE VISITED A WAREHOUSE AND WAS IMPRESSED WITH THE PRODUCTS AND THE OPERATION OF THE COMPANY. HE MADE A PITCH TO THE TEACHERS IN THE BUMS ROOM TO BUY THE STOCK. HE DID CONVINCE SOME TEACHERS TO BUY THAT STOCK. THE BUMS ROOM WAS KNOWN AS A HAVEN FOR MISINFORMATION. BUT ANYWAY, THERE WERE TEACHERS IN THE BUMS ROOM EAGER TO INVEST IN STOCKS THROUGH HIS FIRM. FOR MANY YEARS AFTER, A TEACHER WHO WAS A BUMS ROOM VISITOR COMPLAINED ABOUT PURCHASING THAT STOCK WHICH FELL TO LESS THAN $1. THIS NOT TO SAY THERE WERE NO SUCCESS STORIES. LATER THE BOOK DISCUSSES MANY THINGS AND SERVICES OFFERED IN THE BUMS ROOM.

MR. WILLIAM===LONG TENURED SUPERINTENDANT==SAW THE BUMS ROOM AND SUBMITTED AN APPLICATION FOR MEMBERSHIP.

IT'S POSSIBLE THAT MR. WILLIAM ONLY ENTERED THE BUMS ROOM A COUPLE OF TIMES AFTER THAT. AT THE END OF HIS TIME AS DISTRICT SUPERINTENDANT, HE WAS INVESTIGATED BY A COUPLE OF AGENCIES FOR FRAUDULENT ACTIVITIES. POLITICS IS TOUGH AND TRICKY ON MANY LEVELS. MR. WILLIAM==R.I.P.

MR. AL 3===SECOND APPEARANCE==ARMY VETERAN==THE DRUMMER==OUR VOICE OF DOOM==IT'S NEVER GOING TO BE GOOD.

IT WAS A WEEKEND IN THE AMISH COUNTRY, LANCASTER PA. IT WAS A NICE HOTEL WITH BREAKFAST INCLUDED AND A TOUR OF THE AREA IN A COMFORTABLE NEW VAN. IN ADDITION, THERE WAS AN INDOOR POOL AND MUSIC AT NIGHT, SO THE THREE BUM COUPLES WERE HAVING A GOOD TIME. THEN CAME THE TOUR AFTER BREAKFAST. THE VAN DRIVER WHO WAS ALSO THE TOUR GUIDE TOLD US ABOUT THE THREE MILE ISLAND NUCLEAR PROBLEM AS WE WERE PASSING NEAR IT. THE VOICE OF DOOM POPPED UP WITH WE JUST PASSED EGG FARMS. THE DRIVER SAID WE ATE THE FRESH EGGS FROM THIS AREA THIS MORNING. MR. AL 3 SAID NO WONDER MY STOMACH IS BOTHERING ME. I WON'T EAT ANYMORE EGGS HERE. MR. AL 3 DIDN'T STOP TALKING ABOUT IT. NEXT MORNING MR. AL 3 HAD PANCAKES, PROBABLY MADE WITH EGGS FROM THAT AREA.

MR. MARV===SECOND APPEARANCE==A CLASSIC BUM==KNOWN FOR DIRECT RESPONSES

PRINCIPAL DAVID 2 WALKED INTO THE EAGLE BARBER SHOP AND SAW MR. MARV GETTING A HAIRCUT AND A SHAVE. BACK AT THE SCHOOL, PRINCIPAL DAVID 2 APPROACHED MR. MARV SAYING IT WASN'T LUNCH TIME WHEN YOU WERE IN THE BARBER SHOP. MR. MARV SAID, YOU WERE THERE TOO. MR. MARV WAS GIVEN A LETTER FOR HIS FILE, WHICH RESULTED IN A BIG "STARS OF DAVID" POSTER TACKED ONTO THE BUMS ROOM BULLETIN BOARD. ANYONE GETTING A PRINCIPAL DAVID 2 REPRIMAND LETTER, HAD THEIR NAME WITH A STAR ADDED ONTO THE "STARS OF DAVID" POSTER. NO MORE

LETTERS TO THE BUMS AFTER THE "STARS OF DAVID" POSTER.

MR. LESTER===A SCHOOL CUSTODIAN WHO REALLY CARED

MR. LESTER WAS MOST HOSPITABLE TO THE TEACHERS AND HIS HANDYMAN ASSISTANT. WHEN HIS HOSPITALITY WAS SHARED BY HIS ASSISSTANT, HE WOULD NOT ALLOW HIS ASSISTANT TO FIX ANY WINDOW THAT HAD TO BE OPENED. MR. LESTER HAD THE NICEST WORDS FOR THE TEACHERS AND GREAT RESPECT FOR MR. DAVE HIS #1 HANDYMAN. HE WAS ALSO WELL LIKED IN THE SCHAEFER HOUSE.

## VACATION DAY CAMP SUMMER PROGRAM

Vacation Day Camp

MANY BUMS WORKED THE SUMMER PROGRAM CALLED VACATION DAY CAMP{V.D.C.}. IT WAS AT A V.D.C. SUMMER PROGRAM THAT I BECAME FRIENDS WITH MR. MARIO WHO LATER BECAME THE DISTRICT UNION REPRESENTATIVE AND THEN DISTRICT SUPERINTENDANT.
 THE FIRST YEARS OF THE VACATION DAY CAMP PROGRAM THERE WERE SCHEDULED TRIPS TO AMUSEMENT PARKS, ZOOS AND SPORTING EVENTS. THE HOURS WERE FROM 10AM TO 5PM. IT WAS A FULL DAY PROGRAM WHICH REMINDS ME OF A MR. MARIO AND MR. JERRY PRANK. MR. MARIO AND MR. JERRY WERE THE TEACHERS WHILE MR. FRED WAS TEACHER=IN=CHARGE. MR. FRED WAS A STICKLER ABOUT LEAVING TIME. EVEN THOUGH ALL THE KIDS CLEARED OUT OF THE SCHOOL AND THE EQUIPMENT

WAS PUT AWAY, MR. FRED DID NOT WANT US TO LEAVE BEFORE 5 PM. ONE EVENING MR. MARIO AND MR. JERRY WERE DOING SOMETHING IN THE NEIGHBORHOOD AFTER CLOSING THE VACATION DAY CAMP. SINCE THEY HAD TO BE IN THE NEIGHBORHOOD LATER, AT 4:30 THEY PUT THEIR WATCHES BACK TO 4PM. WHEN 5PM CAME MR. MARIO AND MR. JERRY SHOWED MR. FRED THAT IT WAS ONLY 4:30 ON THEIR WATCHES AND NOT TIME TO GO. THEY ALL STAYED ANOTHER 15 MINUTES AND LEFT AT 5:15PM. MR. FRED DIDN'T BOTHER THEM AGAIN ABOUT LEAVING A FEW MINUTES EARLY WHEN ALL WAS CLEARED AND PUT AWAY.

DURING THE NEW YORK CITY BUDGET CRISIS, THE HOURS WERE CHANGED TO 12PM TO 4PM MONDAY THROUGH THURSDAY. WHEN THE HOURS WERE CUT THERE WERE NO TRIPS TO RYE PLAYLAND, THE BRONX ZOO, NO MORE USING BUSES, ALL TRIPS AND EVENTS WERE IN LOCAL PARKS OR AT OTHER NEIGHBORHOOD SCHOOLS. JUNIOR HIGH SCHOOL 50 HAD A SUMMER SCHOOL PROGRAM FROM 9AM TO 12PM. LUNCH WAS SERVED AT 12PM FOR ALL THE KIDS, SUMMER SCHOOL AND VACATION DAY CAMP KIDS. DURING LUNCH THE ARTS AND CRAFTS ROOM AND THE GYM WERE OPEN. AFTER LUNCH THE CAFETERIA BECAME THE GAMEROOM. THERE WERE PING PONG TABLES, NOK HOCKEY GAMES AND MANY TABLE GAMES. AT TIMES AN EXCITING GAME THAT INVOLVED A REAL MOUSE WAS ADDED. ONCE IN A WHILE A KID WOULD SPOT A MOUSE IN THE LUNCHROOM CAUSING THE BOYS TO CHASE AND TRY TO KICK THE MOUSE. IF THEY COULD GET IT IN A CORNER AGAINST THE WALL, THEY WON THE GAME. THE SIGHT OF A MOUSE WAS NOT UNUSUAL. IT DID NOT CAUSE CONCERN, THE BOYS MADE THE BEST OF IT.

WHEN THE HOURS WERE CUT, THE LUNCH STAFF WAS CUT AND LUNCHES WERE DROPPED OFF AT THE SCHOOL TO BE DISTRIBUTED TO THE STUDENTS. THE TEACHER=IN=CHARGE OF V.D.C. 50 ORDERED MORE LUNCHES THAN THERE WERE KIDS. AFTER THE KIDS ATE, THE PARENTS WOULD BE THERE WITH SHOPPING BAGS TO TAKE HOME THE EXTRA LUNCHES. THIS WAS APPRECIATED BY MANY MOMS IN THE NEIGHBORHOOD.

DEAN SAM WAS THE TEACHER=IN=CHARGE AT THE JUNIOR HIGH SCHOOL 50 VACATION DAY CAMP. MR. ROBERT 1 SUPERVISED THE. SPORTS PROGRAM WHILE MR. JERRY HAD THE KIDS CREATE SOME INTERESTING PROJECTS IN THE ARTS AND CRAFTS ROOM. MR. JERRY HAD A FRIEND IN WILLIAMSBURG THAT ALLOWED HIM TO TAKE SHIPPING CRATE WOOD FROM WHICH THE KIDS MADE PLAQUES. THEY MADE CARTOONS, I LOVE MOM, SPORTS AND OTHER INTERESTING PLAQUES USING PAINT, TILES, PAPER AND GLUE ON THE PIECES OF WOOD.

MR. MARIO AND MR. JERRY WERE THE TWO TEACHERS THAT STARTED THE ANNUAL VACATION DAY CAMP CARNIVAL. AT THE END OF THE FIRST SEASON THAT MR. JERRY AND MR. MARIO WORKED TOGETHER AT V.D.C. 19, THEY SET UP A CARNIVAL IN THE SCHOOL YARD.

MR. MARIO WAS IMPRESSED AND ASKED A SUPERVISOR FROM THE DISTRICT OFFICE TO VIEW THE EVENT. WE HAD TEN ACTIVITIES WITH AN ACTIVITY SHEET FOR EVERY KID. THE ACTIVITIES WERE SIMPLE GAMES LIKE FLIP A BALL INTO A BASKET, SHOOT A BASKETBALL INTO THE HOOP, BOWL DOWN THE 3 SODA BOTTLES, WALK BALANCING A PING PONG BALL ON A SPOON, FLIP

PING PONG BALLS INTO THE CANS, HIT AND TURNOVER THE HANGING PLASTIC BOTTLE AND SOME ROLLING THE BALL GAMES. THERE WERE SIGNS MADE IN THE ARTS AND CRAFTS ROOM. A SIMPLE CARNIVAL CAN OFFER LOTS OF ENJOYMENT TO KIDS. THE GAMES, PRIZES AND ACTIVITY SHEETS IMPRESSED THE SUPERVISORS PROMPTING AN ANNUAL VACATION DAY CAMP CARNIVAL IN CONVENIENT SCHOOL YARDS AT THE END OF EVERY SUMMER. EVERY SCHOOL WAS REQUIRED TO DONATE AN EVENT FOR THE CARNIVAL. OVER THE YEARS MR. MARIO WOULD REMIND ME THAT IT WAS THE TWO OF US THAT STARTED THE ANNUAL VACATION DAY CAMP CARNIVAL.

HERE IS ANOTHER VACATION DAY CAMP MEMORY. OUR SOFTBALL TEAM MADE IT INTO THE CHAMPIONSHIP GAME TO BE PLAYED AT MCCARREN PARK. OUR TEAM HAD NO PLAYER OVER 15 YEARS OLD, AS WERE THE GUIDELINES. THE OTHER TEAM SHOWED UP WITH BEARDS OR A THREE DAY SHADOW. EVERY PLAYER ON THEIR TEAM WAS OVER THE AGE LIMIT. THESE GUYS RAN THE BASES WITH FOOTBALL TECHNIQUES INTIMIDATING THE 14 YEAR OLDS ON OUR TEAM. IT WAS NOT PROPERLY REVIEWED. THE DISTRICT OFFICE SHOULD GET AN "F" FOR NOT HANDLING IT PROPERLY.

## BUMS GROUP 5===*SOME WINNING BUMS*

THIS GROUP IS A MIXTURE OF FIVE THAT AVOIDED HUMOR AND THREE THAT COULD HAVE BEEN SITCOM WRITERS. IN THIS GROUP THREE HAVE ALREADY APPEARED AND FIVE MAKE FIRST APPEARANCE. MOST COULD BE SITCOM COMEDY CHARACTERS. THEY ALL HAD THEIR SPECIAL PLACE IN THE BUMS CLUB.

NO FULL NAMES TO PROTECT THE GUILTY.

MR. S.===PRANKWRITER==BOOK CONTRIBUTOR==WE STILL TALK ON THE PHONE ABOUT THE BUMS AND THE BUMS ROOM==ALWAYS ATTENDED BUMS FUNCTIONS==HE CONTINUES SOCIAL CONTACTS WITH BUMS AND BUMS ROOM VISITORS.

MR. S. LIKED TO WRITE THE PRANK APPLICATIONS. HE TYPED THE BUMS MEMBERSHIP APPLICATION THAT WAS SENT TO MR. WILLIAM, THE DISTRICT SUPERINTENDANT.
HERE IS ONE PRANK THAT GOT OUT OF HAND. MR. DICK CAME TO JUNIOR HIGH SCHOOL 50 EVERYDAY WITH A SHOPPING WAGON LOADED WITH BOOKS IN IT. MR. WARREN THE PRANKERER, ASKED MR. DICK IF HE GOT TO ORDER THIS YEAR'S MUSIC SUPPLIES. MR. DICK GOT EXCITED AND ASKED HOW DO I ORDER THEM. MR. WARREN SAID FORM 232B. MR. DICK ASKED WHERE TO GET THE FORM. MR. S. OFFERED TO GET AN ORDER FORM FOR MR. DICK. MR. S. AND MR. VINNY TYPED UP AN AUTHENTIC LOOKING SUPPLY REQUEST FORM 232B, WHICH INCLUDED MUSIC, SHOP AND HOME ECONOMICS. THEY GAVE ONE TO MR. DICK AND TOLD HIM TO SUBMIT IT TO MRS. G. WHO DEALT WITH SUPPLIES.

MR. DICK TOOK IT HOME, FILLED IT OUT AND SUBMITTED IT TO THE SUPPLY LADY NEXT DAY. THE SUPPLY LADY HAD NO IDEA ABOUT WHAT TO DO WITH IT, SO SHE ASKED THE HOME ECO TEACHER IF SHE GOT ONE. THE HOME ECO TEACHER, UPSET WENT DIRECTLY TO PRINCIPAL FRANK AND ASKED WHAT IS THE REASON THAT SHE DIDN'T GET A SUPPLY REQUEST FORM. THE PRINCIPAL SAID HE KNOWS NOTHING ABOUT IT. AT THIS POINT, FORM 232B INVOLVED SEVEN PEOPLE. MR. WARREN, MR. S., MR. VINNY, THE PRINCIPAL, THE SUPPLY LADY, THE HOME ECO TEACHER, MR. DICK AND WILL INVOLVE DR. SAM AT THE BOARD OF EDUCATION. MR. DICK TOLD MR. S. AND MR. VINNY THAT MRS. G, THE SUPPLY LADY, DOESN'T KNOW WHAT TO DO WITH IT.

MR. WARREN TOLD MR. DICK TO CALL A CONTACT AT THE BOARD OF EDUCATION WHO WILL EXPEDITE IT. THE EXPEDITOR WAS DR. SAM, AN OLD JUNIOR HIGH SCHOOL 50 BUM. DR. SAM WAS OUR SONG AND DANCE PERFORMER IN THE TEACHER TALENT SHOWS. MR. DICK CALLED DR. SAM AT THE BOARD OF EDUCATION WHO TOLD HIM TO ORDER MORE STUFF, HE WILL HAVE EVERYTHING NEXT DAY. THIS CONTINUED FOR DAYS. IT WAS A BUMS ROOM PRANKEROO. IT INVOLVED TOO MANY PEOPLE.

MR. SAM 1===OUR BORN VICTIM MAKES HIS FOURTH APPEARANCE==THE WRONG TOOTH PULLED—FAKE COVERAGE==UNWANTED HUGGING.

MR. SAM 1 LOOKED AT THURSDAYS NEWSPAPER ADS FOR GOOD WEEKEND FOOD PRICES. HE WAS WITH MISS LILLIAN, WHO THE KIDS CALLED BIG BIRD, WHEN HE SAW CHICKEN THIGHS FOR 51 CENTS A POUND. HE TOLD HER ABOUT IT, SO SHE ASKED HIM TO GET TWO PACKAGES FOR HER. NEXT MORNING,

THEY MET AGAIN IN THE GUIDANCE OFFICE, WHERE MR. SAM 1 HANDED THE TWO PACKAGES OF CHICKENS TO HER. SHE TOLD HIM THAT SHE DOESN'T NEED THEM BECAUSE SHE ALREADY BOUGHT THEM YESTERDAY FOR 49 CENTS A POUND IN HER NEIGHBORHOOD. OUR BORN VICTIM WAS HOLDING THE BIRDS, WHILE BIG BIRD WALKED AWAY.

MR. JOE 1=== OUR UNION CHAPTER LEADER==HE DID NOT HAVE AN AFTERNOON HOMEROOM TO DISMISS==EARLY IN, EARLY OUT==HE WAS THE EARLY MORNING COVERAGE DISPENSER.

MR. JOE 1 MANNED THE PHONES BEFORE CLASSES STARTED. IF TEACHERS WERE SICK OR DELAYED, MR. JOE 1 WOULD LOCATE TEACHERS TO COVER THE UNATTENDED CLASSES. GETTING A COVERAGE FROM MR. JOE 1 MEANT A FEW EXTRA DOLLARS AT THE END OF THE MONTH. MR. SAM 1 GOT THAT FAKE COVERAGE SLIP, BUT NOT FROM MR. JOE 1 SO MR. SAM 1 DID NOT GET ANY MONEY EVEN THOUGH HE SPENT THE PERIOD IN THE GYM. SOME TEACHERS LIKED TO TAKE COVERAGES WHILE SOME RATHER NOT GET THEM. MR. JOE 1 TOOK THE EARLY MORNING GIG SO HE COULD LEAVE THE SCHOOL EARLY. SOMETIMES HE COULD BE HOME BEFORE THE AFTERNOON DISMISSAL.

MR. LENNY 1===COULD SLEEP SMOKING A CIGAR==COULD BURN HOLES IN HIS PANTS FROM THE LIT CIGAR ASHES==TEACHERS IN THE BUMS ROOM WOULD WATCH THE CIGAR ASHES FALL ONTO HIS PANTS==BIG TV SPORTS FAN, HE COULD BE UP LATE AT NIGHT==MR. LENNY 1 COULD SLEEP ON A BUMS ROOM CHAIR OR ON THE CHAIR AT HIS DESK DURING CLASSTIME.

WHEN MR. LENNY 1 WOULD FALL ASLEEP IN THE CLASSROOM THE STUDENTS WERE VERY QUIET. SOME NEW TEACHERS WOULD SAY THAT MR. LENNY 1 HAS BETTER CLASS CONTROL SLEEPING, THAN THEY HAVE TRYING TO TEACH THE CLASS. THE NEW TEACHERS ADDED FUN TO THE BUMS ROOM WITH THEIR OBSERVATIONS.

THE BUMS ROOM HAD AN ATTRACTION FOR PEOPLE THAT LIKED TO BE ENTERTAINED OR TO ENTERTAIN OTHERS. MR. LENNY 1 BROUGHT SOME MORNING FUN. HE HELPED FUND RAISING FOR HIS RELIGIOUS ORGANIZATION BY SELLING SCRATCH OFFS. SO, DURING THE MORNING GATHERING IN THE BUMS ROOM, GUYS WERE SCRATCHING. THE ROOM BECAME CROWDED WITH ALL KINDS OF STAFF MEMBERS. THERE WERE TEACHERS, ADMINISTRATORS EVEN A STATE EDUCATION DEPARTMENT REPRESENTATIVE, ALL LOOKING TO HAVE FUN. STATE DEPARTMENT REPRESENTATIVE. LENNY WAS SENT TO JUNIOR HIGH SCHOOL 50 TO OFFER METHODS TO THE MATH TEACHERS TO IMPROVE THE STUDENTS' MATH ABILITY. THE THIRD DAY THAT STATE DEPARTMENT REP. LENNY WAS AT JUNIOR HIGH SCHOOL 50, HE WAS IN THE BUMS ROOM YELLING "I GOT 3 CHERRIES". STATE DEPARTMENT REP. LENNY WAS A WINNER. HE WAS ASSIGNED TO JUNIOR HIGH SCHOOL 50 FOR ONE WEEK. WHEN HE WAS LEAVING, HE LET US KNOW THAT HE WILL MISS THE BUMS ROOM.

MR. MARV===THIRD APPEARANCE==BARTENDER==, MINOR LEAGUE BASEBALL PLAYER==HE SET UP HIS SNEAK SNACK STUDENTS.

MR. MARV COULD FILL A CHAPTER WITH HIS ANTICS AND ATTITUDE. WHEN HE WASN'T ON THE COT, HE LIKED TO READ HIS SPORTS PAPER TO BE ABLE TO MAKE INTELLIGENT BETS.

ON CLERICAL HALF DAYS, A FAVORITE PLACE TO EAT WAS THE PASTRAMI KING WHICH WAS ONE BLOCK AWAY FROM THE SCHOOL. MR. MARV ASKED SOMEONE TO BRING BACK A PASTRAMI SANDWICH AND TWO HOT CHERRY PEPPERS. MR. MURRAY YELLED "ALL YOU CAN EAT IS 2". MR. MURRAY WAS ASKED HOW MANY CAN YOU EAT? MR. MURRAY SAID, "A LOT MORE THAN 2". HE WAS ASKED, CAN YOU EAT TEN? MR. MURRAY SAID, SURE. HE WAS TOLD YOU'RE FULL OF CRAP. MR. MARV ASKED MR. MURRAY IF I BUY THEM WILL YOU EAT THEM? MR. MURRAY SAID, SURE NO PROBLEM. SOME GUYS YELLED YOU'RE NOT GOING TO EAT TEN! MR. MARV OFFERED A CHALLENGE TO COVER ALL $10 BETS AGAINST ANYONE WHO SAYS MR. MURRAY WILL NOT EAT TEN HOT CHERRY PEPPERS. MR. MARV SAID PUT UP YOUR MONEY, HE WILL EAT TEN PEPPERS. THERE WERE FOUR TAKERS FOR THAT BET.

FOUR GUYS PUT THE $10 ON THE TABLE, MR. MARV COVERED THE $40 AND THE GAME WAS ON.
THEY BROUGHT BACK THE FOOD AND THE HOT PEPPERS. MEANWHILE MR. MURRAY WENT TO THE BODEGA ACROSS THE STREET TO GET A CONTAINER OF MILK. IT WAS QUITE A SCENE AROUND THE TABLE IN THE BUMS ROOM. THERE WERE COMMENTS AND CHEERING WITH EACH PEPPER AND DRINK OF MILK THAT MR. MURRAY CONSUMED. YES, MR. MURRAY DOWNED TEN HOT CHERRY PEPPERS, ONE BY ONE, EACH TIME DRINKING SOME MILK AND LOOKING LIKE HE WILL NOT MAKE IT. HE LOOKED IN PAIN BUT WITH COACH MR. MARV PUSHING HIM TO DO IT, MURRAY PUSHED HIMSELF. MR. MURRAY DID SWALLOW TEN PEPPERS. MR. MARV GAVE HIM $20, THE OTHER $20 PAID FOR THE SANDWICH AND THE PEPPERS. MR. MURRAY RAN OUT OF THE ROOM. IT WAS A GREAT BUMS ROOM EVENT. BY THE WAY, MR.

MURRAY WAS NOT IN SCHOOL FOR THE NEXT TWO DAYS.

MR. WARREN===PRANKERER==THIRD APPEARANCE==COULD BE A TV COMEDY WRITER==HIS SHIRT PRANK DREW A CROWD.

MR. WARREN ADDED THIS BEAUTY TO HIS LIST OF PRANKS. MR. LENNY 1 WORE THIS LIVELY RED AND WHITE CHECKERED SHIRT. MR. WARREN TOOK A PHOTO AND SENT THE PHOTO TO HAVE A BIG JIGSAW PUZZLE MADE OF THE SHIRT. AT AN OPPORTUNE TIME, GUYS GOT AROUND THE BUMS ROOM TABLE AS SOME GUYS WORKED ON THE PUZZLE. IT WAS FUN WATCHING MR. LENNY 1 SHAKING HIS HEAD AS HE SAW HIS SHIRT DEVELOP BIG AND BRIGHT. ALL HE KEPT SAYING WAS, HE HAS MONEY TO WASTE, HE HAS MONEY TO WASTE. THE ONLOOKERS GOT A KICK OUT OF IT. WITH MR. WARREN YOU DIDN'T KNOW WHAT'S COMING NEXT.

DR. SAM===SOCIALIZED WITH ADMINISTRATORS==LIKED TO GRAB A SMOKE==TEACHER TALENT SHOW SONG AND DANCE MAN==GOT TO WORK AT THE CENTRAL BOARD.

DR. SAM SHARED AN OFFICE WITH ASSISTANT PRINCIPAL PHIL WHEN DR. SAM HAD THE QUOTA POSITION OF SCHOOL ACCOUNTS. HE WOULD HIDE ASSISTANT PRINCIPAL PHIL'S PAPERS BECAUSE HE ENJOYED FRUSTRATING HIM. DR. SAM SPENT TEACHING TIME WITH ONE FOOT IN THE HALL AND ONE FOOT IN THE CLASSROOM. DID HE DO THIS WHEN HE WAS OBSERVED BY THE ADMINISTRATOR? DR. SAM AND MR. VINNY PERFORMED THE SKIT, "ME AND MY SHADOW" WITH TOP HAT AND CANE IN THE TEACHERS TALENT SHOW.

MR. BARRY===SET HIS SIGHTS ON LAWYERING

THE BUMS ROOM HAD PLENTY OF LAWYERS. MR. BARRY BECAME A REAL ONE. HE WAS THE DEFENSE ATTORNEY FOR A BUMS CLUB MEMBER. THE DECISION WAS FAVORABLE FOR THE BUM.

## THE TEACHER TALENT SHOW==ABOVE AND BEYOND

A NUMBER OF THE BUMS PERFORMED IN THE TEACHER TALENT SHOWS. MR. LEONARD, DR. SAM, MR. ROBERT 1, MR. SID 1 AND MR. JERRY DID IT EVERY YEAR WHILE MR. PETE 1, MR. BEN 1, MR. ARTIE 1, MR. VINNY AND OTHERS MADE SPORADIC APPEARANCES. FOR YEARS, MR. SID 1 APPEARED IN HIS GOLD JACKET SINGING CUANTO CALIENTE EL SOL WHILE MR. LEONARD PUT ON A BIG BLONDE WIG TO BELLOW OUT SOMETHING FROM THE TWENTIES. DR. SAM DID A SONG AND DANCE ROUTINE AND MR. ROBERT 1 WORE A CAPE SINGING DUKE, DUKE, DUKE, DUKE OF EARL. MR. JERRY DID HIS HARMONICA ROUTINE ACCOMPANIED WITH MR. EARL, THE MUSIC MAN, ON THE PIANO. WHEN THESE GUYS DID AN APPEARANCE, THEY REALLY ENTERTAINED. MR. PETE 1 HAD A GREAT VOICE DOING A BALLAD, MR. BEN 1 DID A READING OF A POEM, MR. ARTIE 1 PLAYED AN ACCORDIAN AND MR. VINNY ACCOMPANIED DR. SAM DOING A SONG AND DANCE ROUTINE.

THE STUDENTS LOVED OBSERVING ANOTHER SIDE OF THEIR TEACHERS. WHEN SPEAKING WITH PAST STUDENTS, MANY REMEMBER THE TEACHERS PERFORMING IN THOSE TEACHER TALENT SHOWS. IT IS INTERESTING THAT YEAR AFTER YEAR, JUST ABOUT EVERY TEACHER TALENT SHOW PERFORMER WAS A MEMBER OF THE BUMS CLUB. BUMS CLUB MEMBERS TAKE A BOW.

Teacher Talent Show

## BUMS GROUP 6===*BUMS, BUMS, BUMS*

NINE BUMS ARE COVERED IN THIS GROUP. MAYBE ONLY A FEW WOULD BE SITCOM MATERIAL, BUT THEY ALL WERE GOOD BUMS. THE WHEELER DEALER, WHO EVENTUALLY BECAME THE DISTRICT SUPERINTENDANT HELPING TEACHERS IN DIFFICULT SITUATIONS WAS QUITE A CHARACTER. TEACHERS WHO WANTED TO BE ADMINISTRATORS WOULD FOLLOW HIM LIKE HE WAS A FAMOUS STAR. THESE TEACHERS FORMED HIS SQUAD THAT DID THE FOOTWORK TO ELECT THE LOCAL SCHOOL BOARD. THIS GROUP FILLS OUT THE 30+ BUMS PRESENTED IN GROUPS 1 THROUGH GROUP 6.

NO FULL NAMES TO PROTECT THE GUILTY.

PRINCIPAL FRANK===JUNIOR HIGH SCHOOL 50 PRINCIPAL 15 YEARS==INSTEAD OF AN ACTING CAREER==BLENDED INTO THE JHS 50 FABRIC.

AT TIMES PRINCIPAL FRANK PARTICIPATED IN THE HALF DAY POKER GAMES. HE PROVIDED THE MATCHES FOR THE MR. DICK TIE BURNING CEREMONY. PRODUCED AND DIRECTED THE SHOW "ARSENIC AND OLD LACE" WHICH PLAYED THREE NIGHTS FOR THE DISTRICT 14 COMMUNITY. MANY BUMS PARTICIPATED IN THE SHOW, TAKING LEAD OR SUPPORTING ROLES, EVEN SELLING TICKETS FOR THE SHOW. IT WAS FILLED TO CAPACITY, BRAVO!!

MR. MARIO===DISTRICT REPRESENTATIVE OF THE UNITED FEDERATION OF TEACHERS==WANTED MEMBERSHIP IN THE BUMS CLUB==PART OF THE MEDIATION TEAM IN THE MR. SAM 1 HUGGING THE SPEECH TEACHER INCIDENT WHICH RESULTED IN NO CONSEQUENCES TO BUM SAM 1.

A TEACHER LEFT WITHOUT NOTIFYING THE SCHOOL. HIS PERSONAL REASONS KEPT HIM AWAY FOR ABOUT TWO YEARS. MR. MARIO AND MR. JERRY TRIED TO CONTACT HIM BUT HE WOULD NOT ANSWER OR RETURN THE PHONE CALLS. WHEN HE RETURNED TO BROOKLYN, HE CALLED ASSISSTANT PRINCIPAL BERNIE, ASKING TO WORK AGAIN AT JUNIOR HIGH SCHOOL 50. ASSISSTANT PRINCIPAL BERNIE SPOKE WITH MR. JERRY ABOUT THE REQUEST. MR. JERRY CONTACTED MR. MARIO WHO QUICKLY UTTERED SOME EXPLITIVES ABOUT HIM NOT ANSWERING THE CALLS. HE DID ANSWER MR. MARIO'S NEXT CALL AND WAS BACK AT JUNIOR HIGH SCHOOL 50 FOR MANY, MANY YEARS. BUMS HELPING ANOTHER BUM.

FOR SOME REASON JUNIOR HIGH SCHOOL 50 PICKED UP SIXTH GRADE CLASSES WITH TEACHERS FROM ANOTHER SCHOOL. BECAUSE OF THIS, SOME JUNIOR HIGH SCHOOL 50 TEACHERS WERE TRANSFERRED TO OTHER SCHOOLS. MR. CHAIM, A JUNIOR HIGH SCHOOL 50 MATH TEACHER, WAS QUITE DISSATISFIED AT THE NEW PLACE. MR. MARIO CAME TO THE RESCUE. A BUM'S PHONE CALL TO MR. MARIO RESULTED IN MR. CHAIM BACK TEACHING MATH AT JUNIOR HIGH SCHOOL 50. MR. CHAIM HAS THE DISTINCTION OF EVERY STUDENT IN HIS CLASS PASSING THE ALGEBRA REGENT. MR. MARIO ALSO WAS INSTRUMENTAL IN BRINGING OTHER TEACHERS BACK TO JUNIOR HIGH SCHOOL 50.

MR. GIL===ORIGINAL BUM==SET UP THE FIRST BIG BUMS BASH.

ADVANCED TO SUPERINTENDANT OF SCHOOLS OUTSIDE NEW YORK CITY. HE ALWAYS SAID, THE BUMS OF JUNIOR HIGH SCHOOL 50 WAS A GREAT

TEACHING STAFF. HE WOULD HAVE LIKED TO HAVE THIS STAFF IN THE SCHOOLS THAT HE SUPERVISED.

MR. PETE 1===SECOND APPEARANCE==ATE HIS LUNCH IN THE MORNING AS SOON AS HE CAME INTO THE BUMS ROOM==LIKED TO DECORATE OUR WALLS.

AFTER THE STAFF WAS INTRODUCED TO THE NEW EXPERIMENTAL GATES READING PROGRAM MR. PETE 1 HUNG AN OLD RUSTY GATE ON THE BUMS ROOM WALL.

MR. LENNY 1 TOLD HIS ARMY STORY AS A TANK OPERATOR. THIS PROMPTED MR. PETE 1 TO STOP INTO THE NEIGHBORHOOD RECRUITING OFFICE TO GET SOME POSTERS SHOWING A TANK. MR. PETE 1 WROTE MR. LENNY'S NAME ON THE POSTERS AND TAPED THEM ON THE BUMS ROOM WALL. ANOTHER WALL DECORATION BY MR. PETE 1 WAS HIS CREATIVE EYE CHART USING THE SIX LETTERS OF THE NEW PRINCIPAL'S NAME. THIS CHART WAS PLACED ON A WALL EASY FOR EVERYONE TO SEE AND LAUGH. THIS WAS AN EYE CATCHER.

ROBERT 2===LAST "ORIGINAL" BUM TO TEACH AT JUNIOR HIGH SCHOOL 50==HAS INTERESTING MEMORIES OF MANY BUMS==A GREAT BOOK CONTRIBUTOR.

THIS BOOK HAS MANY CONTRIBUTIONS PROVIDED BY ROBERT 2. AFTER A MEETING WITH A PARENT, CINDY {THE STUDENT} ASKED MR. ROBERT 2 TO LOOK AT HER MOTHER WALKING DOWN THE HALL BECAUSE SHE HAS A REAL NICE ASS.

DEAN SAM===SECOND APPEARANCE==LONGEST TENURED JUNIOR HIGH SCHOOL 50 DEAN==HAD A

PADDLE LABELLED BOARD OF EDUCATION==HIS STRENGTH HELPED LIFT THE REAR END OF A SMALL CAR POSITIONING IT TO CHANGE A TIRE.

THE VACATION DAY CAMP PROGRAM WAS IN FULL SWING IN JULY. DEAN SAM WAS THE TEACHER IN CHARGE, MR. ROBERT 1 RAN THE GYM AND SOFTBALL PROGRAM WHILE MR. JERRY SUPERVISED ARTS AND CRAFTS. THE DEAN'S OFFICE WAS USED AS THE VACATION DAY CAMP OFFICE DURING THE SUMMER. A STUDENT WALKED INTO THE OFFICE SAYING HE WANTS TO PAY THE THREE THAT HE OWES. SHARKEY CAME TO GET THREE PADDLE WHACKS SO HE COULD PARTICIPATE IN THE GYM.
DEAN SAM TOOK THE PADDLE OFF THE NAIL ON THE WALL. SHARKEY LEANED AGAINST THE DESK WAITING FOR THE PADDLE TO HIT HIS BACKSIDE. DEAN SAM GAVE HIM ONE RAP AND WAIVED THE OTHER TWO BECAUSE SHARKEY APPEARED ON HIS OWN. SHARKEY AND THE DEAN SPOKE A BIT AND THEN PROCEEDED TO THE GYM. DEAN SAM HAD A SPECIAL CONNECTION WITH MANY STUDENTS.

THE STORY WAS, IF A STUDENT WAS MISBEHAVING, SOME PARENTS GAVE DEAN SAM PERMISSION TO PADDLE THE STUDENT'S BACKSIDE. ON THE JUNIOR HIGH SCHOOL 50 SITE, JUNIOR, CARLITO, AND ANTHONY, RESPONDED ABOUT GETTING PADDLED. SANDRA, SAID MR. SAM 2 {WHO ALSO HAD BEEN A DEAN} AND DEAN SAM WERE AWESOME. ANNIE WROTE EVERYONE WAS SCARED OF HIM BUT NOT ME, HE WAS COOL. JOE. SAID HE HAD TO DEAL WITH SOME OF THE WORST KNUCKLEHEADS OF THE SOUTHSIDE. FABIOLA, WROTE, HE WAS NO JOKE. DARLENE OFFERED, DEAN SAM WAS THE BEST DEAN AND AN AWESOME PERSON.

TEACHERS AGREED, WHEN HIS VOICE WAS HEARD, KIDS FELT SAFE AND TEACHERS DIDN'T HAVE TO BE DISCIPLINARIANS.     DEAN SAM==R.I.P.

MR. PHIL===LOVED THE BUMS ROOM==WAS FAST TO BECOME BUMS PRESIDENT
NEVER SAW HIM COME INTO THE ROOM WITH BOOKS OR MATERIALS. HE WAS ALWAYS HAPPY HANGING OUT. IT SEEMED LIKE HE DIDN'T OWN A TIE OR PANTS WITH NO RIPS. HE WAS A LIKEABLE GUY. HE WAS APPOINTED BUMS PRESIDENT BECAUSE HE DIDN'T CARE.

MR. MEL===A GREAT BUM==DESIGNED THE BUM PIN==LED THE BASKETBALL SESSIONS==HAD GREAT BUMS ROOM IDEAS.

MR. MEL CAME INTO THE BUMS ROOM ANNOUNCING THAT BECAUSE OF AN INTRODUCTORY OFFER HE RECEIVED THREE PORNO FILMS FOR $16. AFTER SOME DISCUSSION TWO OTHER BUMS WERE INTERESTED IN A THREEWAY EXCHANGE DEAL. THE OTHER TWO GUYS WOULD GO FOR THE THREE FILM INTRODUCTORY OFFER. THIS WOULD GIVE EACH GUY NINE FILMS TO WATCH AFTER THE EXCHANGES WERE MADE.
WHEN THE DAY CAME FOR THE FILM EXCHANGE, THE SCHOOL PROJECTOR APPEARED IN THE BUMS ROOM. THE LIGHTS WERE SHUT AND THE PORNO FILM WAS SHOWN ON THE WALL ABOVE THE DIRTY COT. THE SCHOOL SECRETARIES WERE ALERTED TO KNOCK ON THE DOOR BEFORE ENTERING. ONE BUM WAS POSTED TO GUARD THE DOOR. SOME BUMS TRIED TO DISCUSS THE EDUCATIONAL VALUE OF THE FILM. SOME TRIED TO RELATE THE MATERIAL TO A CLASS SUBJECT.

THE SHOWING OF THE FILMS WAS SHORT LIVED, BUT THE SECRETARIES CONTINUED TO KNOCK BEFORE ENTERING THE BUMS ROOM.

MISS MARIE===GIRLS CHILD CARE SHOP TEACHER==OSTRACIZED BY THE OTHER FEMALE SHOP TEACHERS.

THE ONLY FEMALE MEMBER OF THE BUMS CLUB. AFTER DONATING A NEW RED AND WHITE TABLECLOTH TO COVER OUR UNSITELY TABLE, SHE WAS VOTED UNANIMOUSLY INTO THE BUMS CLUB. MARIE CRIED AT THE CEREMONY. MR. GERRY, A GYM TEACHER, LAUGHED SO HARD HE FELL OFF HIS CHAIR.

## BUMS SOCIALIZING

BUMS at Rockefeller Center

THE BUMS CLUB MEMBERS SOCIALIZED OUTSIDE OF SCHOOL IN MANY WAYS. WE MET TO PLAY SOFTBALL IN A SCHOOL YARD ON WEEKENDS IN THE SPRING. LITTLE GROUPS WENT TO SPORTING EVENTS, BIG GROUPS JOINED TOGETHER FOR OUR BUMS BASHES AT THE DOUGLASTON MANOR IN QUEENS, NEW YORK. LITTLE CLIQUES FORMED FOR ALL KINDS OF SOCIALIZING GROUPS.

THERE WAS SOCIALIZING WITH WIVES, OR FRIENDS AT PARKS, OR GATHERINGS AT EACH OTHERS' HOMES. AT MR. JOHN'S HOME THE BUMS GOT TO SEE HIS PAINTING TALENT THAT WAS DISPLAYED ON HIS WALLS. MR. MEL HAD SPECIAL FILMS AT HIS GET TOGETHERS. MR. VINNY LIKED TO BARBEQUE. MR. WARREN WAS KNOWN FOR WEEKEND CARD GAMES.

AT THE HOME OF MR. JERRY ALL ENJOYED THE GREAT COOKING BY HIS WIFE, RHODA.

ONE COLD WINTER NIGHT THERE WAS A GET TOGETHER AT MR. JERRY'S HOUSE. MR. SID 1 PICKED UP BOSS GENE IN HIS NEW CAR. BOSS GENE WAS THE FRONT SEAT PASSENGER. WHEN THE TWO COUPLES ARRIVED AT MR. JERRY'S HOUSE, BOSS GENE TOLD US THE TRIP WAS NO FUN, HIS LEGS WERE FREEZING. THEY DISCOVERED THAT THE AIR CONDITIONER WAS ON. MR. SID 1 WAS JUST LEARNING ABOUT HIS NEW CAR. MR. STEVE HAD POOL PARTIES FOR SOME OF THE TEACHERS. MR. BEN 1, MR. S., MR. STANLEY AND MANY OTHERS CONTINUED TO MEET SOCIALLY.

PLAYING SOFTBALL ON WEEKENDS WITH THE GUYS WAS ESPECIALLY FUN. IN THE SPRING THE BUMS WOULD MEET IN A SCHOOLYARD MAKING BELIEVE THEY WERE ATHLETES. MR. GERRY WHO WAS A GYM TEACHER AND A COLLEGE BASEBALL STAR, SHOWED UP TO PLAY ONE TIME. AFTER SEEING THE LEVEL OF OUR PLAYING, HE SAID, AT LEAST THESE GUYS ARE GREAT TEACHERS. WE ACTUALLY PLAYED SOME GOOD GAMES AGAINST A TEAM IN LINCOLN TERRACE PARK IN BROOKLYN. YEARS LATER A YOUNGER TEACHER TRANSFERRED TO JUNIOR HIGH SCHOOL 50 FROM THE NEIGHBORING JUNIOR HIGH SCHOOL 126. HE HEARD THAT THE BUMS PLAYED SOFTBALL IN THE PAST. HE CHALLENGED JUNIOR HIGH SCHOOL 50 TO A GAME. ALTHOUGH HE WORKED AT JUNIOR HIGH SCHOOL 50 NOW, HE CHOSE TO PLAY WITH HIS OLD SCHOOL. ON AVERAGE WE WERE 20 YEARS OLDER THAN THE JUNIOR HIGH SCHOOL 126 PLAYERS. AFTER THE FIRST INNING IT WAS J.H.S. 126 (4) TO J.H.S. 50 (0). AFTER THE SECOND INNING THE SCORE WAS J.H.S. 126 (11) TO J.H.S. 50 (1). THE GAME CONTINUED FOR ANOTHER TWO INNINGS WITHOUT

KEEPING SCORE. BEFORE THIS GAME THE BUMS HAD NOT PLAYED SOFTBALL FOR A LONG TIME AND AFTER THIS THEY NEVER PLAYED AGAIN.

THE BUMS DID CONTINUE THEIR ACTIVITIES IN THE GYM FOR MANY YEARS. BASKETBALL GAMES AND MARTIAL ARTS DRILLS TOOK PLACE BEFORE CLASSES STARTED AND ON CLERICAL DAYS. MR. JOHN, MR. MARV, MR. MARTY, MR. STEVE, MR. ROBERT 1, MR. GERRY, MR. EDDIE, MR. STANLEY, MR. BEN 1, MR. DON, MR. ARMANDO. AND OTHERS LED BY MR. MEL ENJOYED PLAYING BASKETBALL IN THE GYM. TEACHERS THAT WERE NOT BUMS CLUB MEMBERS JOINED THEM TO PLAY FULL COURT.
MARTIAL ARTS CLASSES LED BY MR. ROBERT 1. AND MR. STANLEY WOUND UP BEING CO=ED WHEN FEMALES JOINED THE GROUP.

THE SOCIALIZING WENT IN ALL DIFFERENT DIRECTIONS. MANY DAYS BUMS WOULD MEET TO WALK IN MANHATTAN OR SPEND TIME AT A MUSEUM. AT MUSEUMS THAT HAD A SUGGESTED PER PERSON DONATION OF $10, WE WOULD SAY "WE ARE NEW YORKERS" AND ONE OF US WOULD DONATE $5 FOR ADMISSION FOR THE WHOLE GROUP.
THE GUYS WOULD HAVE A NIGHT OUT AT THE N.Y. METS GAME. AT ONE OF THE GAMES MR. FRANK 1 SHOWED US THAT HE HAD A GUN PERMIT. HE DIDN'T ONLY SHOW US THE PERMIT. WE ALL DIDN'T THINK A GUN WAS ALLOWED AT THE STADIUM.

THERE WAS AN ADVERTISEMENT FOR A LIVE BURLESQUE SHOW IN A QUEENS THEATRE. THE BUMS JUMPED ON IT. AFTER EATING DINNER IN AN ITALIAN RESTAURANT, WE ALL GOT TO THE THEATRE WHICH WAS ALMOST EMPTY. WE SAT CENTER AISLE IN THE FIRST TWO ROWS. THE SHOW WAS PLENTY

OF FUN UNTIL THE STAR PERFORMER FEATURED BUBBLES THAT FLOATED ALL OVER THE PEOPLE SEATED IN THE FRONT ROWS. THE BUBBLES HAD A PUNGENT PERFUME SMELL THAT PERMEATED OUR CLOTHES AND OUR CARS WHEN WE DROVE HOME.

ANOTHER BUMS SOCIALIZING EVENT WAS WHEN PRINCIPAL FRANK, USED HIS THEATRE EXPERIENCE PRESENTING THE SHOW "ARSENIC AND OLD LACE" TO THE COMMUNITY. THE BUMS PARTICIPATED IN MANY WAYS, MAIN AND SUPORTING ROLES, BUILDING THE SET, SELLING TICKETS AND SEATING GUESTS. THE BUMS WERE HAPPY TO BE PART OF THE THEATRE GROUP. THE SHOW WAS SUCCESSFUL WITH GREAT REVIEWS.

BUMS in Lower Manhattan

## BUMS ROOM GUESTS==*STORIES AND MORE*

HERE'S A CUTE STORY. AN E.S.L. (ENGLISH SECOND LANGUAGE) TEACHER CAME INTO THE BUMS ROOM AND RELATED THIS TO US. ON A TEST ASKING TO FILL IN THE BLANKS, THE FIRST QUESTION WAS---
_____? _____ IS THE VICE PRESIDENT OF THE UNITED STATES. THE TEACHER SAID, MANY OF THE STUDENTS WROTE "WHO". HE SAID MAYBE IT SHOULD BE MARKED CORRECT.

JUNIOR HIGH SCHOOL 50 HAD ABOUT TWENTY FIVE FEMALE STAFF MEMBERS. SOME HAD THEIR CLIQUES THAT WOULD MEET DURING UNASSIGNED PERIODS. THEY WOULD MEET FOR COFFEE, LUNCH, OR GO SHOPPING AT THE NEIGHBORHOOD STORES. THERE WERE SOME WOMEN THAT WERE SORT OF OSTRACISED BY THE GROUPS OF FEMALE TEACHERS. SOME WHO WERE NOT PART OF ANY GROUP WOULD COME INTO THE BUMS ROOM.

MRS. SYLVIA WHO THE PRINCIPAL SOMETIMES REFERRED TO AS A "TOUGH OL' BIRD", WOULD PLOP HERSELF DOWN ON A FLATTENED OLD SOFA CHAIR. WHEN WE NOTICED HER READY TO ENTER THE BUMS ROOM, WE WOULD GET READY FOR THE BOUNCE. WHEN SHE PLOPPED HERSELF DOWN, ALL OF THE BUMS WOULD FLY UP IN THE AIR. MRS. SYLVIA WOULD SAY "YOU GUYS ARE CRAZY".

FOR LESS THAN A YEAR THERE WAS A BIG VENDING MACHINE WITH CANDY AND LITTLE PACKS OF COOKIES IN THE BUMS ROOM. ONE DAY I WALKED INTO THE ROOM AND SAW MRS. SYLVIA WITH THE WINDOW POLE, SHOVING IT INTO THE OPENING OF THE CANDY MACHINE. SHE SAID THAT SHE PUT

MONEY IN AND THE COOKIES DIDN'T COME OUT. SHE WAS THE ONLY ONE IN THE ROOM SO I LEFT. THE NEXT DAY THE VENDING MACHINE WAS BROKEN. FROM THE LITTLE THAT I SAW, MRS. SYLVIA COULD HAVE BEEN AN OLYMPIC JAVELON WINNER.

MISS LILLIAN, A TYPING TEACHER NOT INVOLVED WITH A GROUP OF STAFF MEMBERS WOULD PARK HERSELF IN THE BUMS ROOM. SHE WAS VERY TALL, WORE UNSTYLISH HEELED SHOES AND WALKED LIKE HER FEET WERE HURTING. THE STUDENTS CALLED HER "BIG BIRD". ONE MORNING SHE WAS CONFERRING WITH A PARENT IN A GUIDANCE OFFICE CUBICLE WHEN THE PARENT FELL ASLEEP. MISS LILLIAN KEPT TALKING WHILE HE WAS IN A DEEP SLEEP. FINALLY, SHE TOOK THE NEWSPAPER AND READ IT UNTIL HE WOKE UP. ONE WEEKEND THE TYPING ROOM WAS ROBBED OF THE TYPEWRITERS AND MISS LILLIAN TRANSFERRED TO ANOTHER SCHOOL. THIS SAVED MR. SAM 1 THE PROBLEM OF BUYING CHICKENS FOR HER.

A COMPLETELY DIFFERENT BUMS ROOM VISITOR STORY. MISS DEBBIE WAS A DAY TO DAY SUBSTITUTE TEACHER. SHE LIKED COMING TO JUNIOR HIGH SCHOOL 50 TO HANGOUT IN THE BUMS ROOM. SHE STRAIGHT OUT MADE IT KNOWN THAT SHE HAD EYES FOR ONE OF THE GUYS THAT HUNGOUT IN THE BUMS ROOM. THIS GUY WAS A TALL, GOODLOOKING GUY THAT SOCIALIZED WITH ANOTHER FEMALE TEACHER IN JUNIOR HIGH SCHOOL 50. MISS DEBBIE LET EVERYONE KNOW THAT SHE HAD A DESIRE TO BE WITH HIM. IT WAS INTERESTING TO WATCH HER IN THE BUMS ROOM EVERYTIME THE DOOR OPENED. THERE WERE ALL KINDS OF EMOTIONS SHOWN IN THE BUMS ROOM.

AN ATTENDANCE TEACHER (TRUANT OFFICER} WOULD COME INTO THE BUMS ROOM TO SAY HELLO TO THE GUYS AND GRAB SOME TIME ON THE OLD WORNOUT COT. MR. C.ARL LIKED TO RECLINE AND TALK TO THE GUYS. HE MUST HAVE LIKED TO GO INTO THE MAIN OFFICE BECAUSE HE EVENTUALLY MARRIED THE TALL BLOND SECRETARY. MONTHS LATER WHENEVER MR. CARL CAME TO JUNIOR HIGH SCHOOL 50, THIS IS THE STORY HE TOLD. HE DATED THE SECRETARY FOR A FEW MONTHS. SHE HAD A SON THAT WAS NOT LIVING WITH HER. MR. CARL SAID HE HARDLY SAW THE BOY. MR. CARL AND THE SECRETARY MARRIED AND MR. CARL WOUND UP ADOPTING THE BOY. THE MARRIAGE WAS SHORT LIVED RESULTING IN HIS TIRADE EACH TIME HE VISITED THE BUMS ROOM. I NEVER GOT TO KNOW THE KID, NOW I HAVE TO SUPPORT HIM UNTIL HE'S 21 YEARS OLD. I'M RESPONSIBLE FOR THIS KID 'TIL HE'S 21, THAT'S A LOT OF YEARS. THE BIG BLOND SECRETARY WAS AT JUNIOR HIGH SCHOOL 50 FOR A SHORT TIME. THE BUMS COMMENTS WHEN MR. CARL VISITED THE ROOM CAME FROM ALL DIFFERENT ANGLES.

A TEACHER, WHO WASN'T IN THE BUMS CLUB, OFTEN CAME INTO THE ROOM. HE WAS A COFFEE CLUB MEMBER AND LIKED TO LISTEN TO THE COMMENTS THAT WENT BACK AND FORTH. HE WOULD ALWAYS HAVE AN OPENED BOOK IN HIS HANDS, PRETENDING TO BE READING. EVERY ONCE IN A WHILE, HE WOULD BE ASKED WHY HE NEVER TURNED THE PAGE. HE WOULD SMILE AND EASE HIS WAY OUT OF THE BUMS ROOM. MR. PETE 2, A RELATIVELY NEW TEACHER AT JUNIOR HIGH SCHOOL 50, WOULD JOKE "YOU HAVE THE BOOK UPSIDE DOWN". IT SEEMS HE LIKED TO LISTEN, BUT NOT TO TALK. HE WAS NOT AN OPEN BOOK.

A GUY THAT LIVED IN MANHATTAN LIKED TO WORK AS A SUBSTITUTE TEACHER AT JUNIOR HIGH SCHOOL 50. HE LIKED TALKING SPORTS WITH SOME OF THE GUYS. IN THE BUMS ROOM MR. BOB WAS KNOWN FOR TWO THINGS, SPORTS TRIVIA AND FOR ADMISSION TO VARIOUS EVENTS IN NEW YORK CITY WHERE HE GOT TO EAT AND DRINK FOR FREE. HE LOVED THE PARTIES AT THE UNITED NATIONS. HOW DID HE GET IN? WHY WAS HE ADMITTED? HE HAD IN HIS POSSESION A GROUP OF CARDS THAT IDENTIFIED HIM IN SOME WAY TO ALLOW HIM ADMITTANCE. HE HAD BUSINESS CARDS, PROFESSIONAL CARDS, CARDS THAT FIT THE ADVERTISED EVENT OF THE EVENING. HE SHOWED A LAWYER'S CARD, A TRAVEL AGENT CARD, AN ART APPRAISER, AN ART CONSULTANT CARD, A UNITED FEDERATION OF TEACHERS CARD, A DIPLOMAT CARD, ANY CARD TO FIT THE EVENT. AFTER WORKING AS A SUBSTITUTE TEACHER, MR. BOB WOULD DRESS UP FOR THE EVENT, EVEN PUTTING ON A TUXEDO. THIS GUY'S STORIES AND ESCAPADES WERE PRETTY INTERESTING. MR. BOB WAS ALWAYS WELCOMED TO THE BUMS ROOM.

AN ESL (ENGLISH SECOND LANGUAGE} TEACHER AND HIS 19 YEAR SON JUST BOUGHT A NEW CAR. MR. RAY TOLD US THEY WERE LOOKING FORWARD TO THE DRIVE TO FLORIDA TO VISIT RELATIVES DURING THE HOLIDAY BREAK. AFTER THE HOLIDAY MR. RAY CAME INTO THE BUMS ROOM AND WAS ASKED ABOUT THE TRIP. HE SAID THEY NEVER GOT TO FLORIDA. MR. RAY TOLD US THEY GOT LOST IN STATEN ISLAND. THEY COULDN'T FIND THE RIGHT ROAD SO THEY WENT BACK HOME. MR. RAY SAID THEY USED THE CAR EVERYDAY IN BROOKLYN AND LIKED IT MUCH.

OVER THE YEARS, PROBABLY WITHOUT ANY BUMS REQUEST SOME KIND OF MACHINE WAS PLACED IN THE BUMS ROOM. NONE WAS THERE MORE THAN A YEAR. THERE WAS A SODA MACHINE, A CANDY MACHINE AND A REFRIGERATOR. TEACHERS WOULD STORE THEIR FOOD IN THE REFRIGERATOR IN THE MORNING. A PROBLEM DEVELOPED WHEN ONE LUNCH WAS REMOVED BY SOMEONE THAT DID NOT STORE ANY FOOD IN THAT REFRIGERATOR. IT WAS VERY FUNNY WHEN A TEACHER CAME IN LOOKING FOR HIS LUNCH AND IT WAS GONE. SOMEONE ELSE WAS EATING IT. WE THINK THE CULPRIT WAS DISCOVERED WHEN HE WAS CHALLENGED WALKING OUT WITH SOMEONE ELSE'S LUNCH. THE GUY SAID, "IT LOOKED LIKE MINE, SOME ONE MUST HAVE TAKEN MY LUNCH". THIS GUY MUST HAVE FELT IF HE'S HUNGRY THERE'S A FREE LUNCH AVAILABLE FOR HIM IN THAT REFRIGERATOR. AFTER HE WAS CONFRONTED LUNCHES DIDN'T DISAPPEAR FOR A WHILE.

THERE WAS A TEACHER THAT VISITED THE BUMS ROOM WITH THE IDEA OF QUICK IN AND QUICK OUT. HE WOULD SNEAK A CUP OF COFFEE A FEW TIMES A WEEK. ONLY A FEW COFFEE CLUB MEMBERS WOULD SHOW CONCERN ABOUT HIM TAKING COFFEE WITHOUT BEING A PAYING MEMBER. ONE DAY BOSS GENE CONFRONTED HIM, "IF YOU DON'T WANT TO CONTRIBUTE ANY MONEY, YOU HAVE NO RIGHT TO TAKE COFFEE". THE NEXT DAY MR. LEON CAME INTO THE BUMS ROOM WITH TWO POCKETS FULL OF PLASTIC SPOONS. WHILE HE PUT THE SPOONS ON THE TABLE HE SAID, "I'LL BRING SPOONS, SO I CAN TAKE COFFEE ONCE IN A WHILE". MR. LEON HAD A REPUTATION FOR FILLING HIS SUIT JACKET POCKETS WITH THE KIDS' CONTAINERS OF MILK. HE WAS ALSO ACCUSED OF TAKING TOILET PAPER FROM THE MEN'S

BATHROOM. THERE WERE CHARACTERS VISITING THE BUMS ROOM, SOME WERE STAYERS AND SOME HAD REASONS TO GET OUT QUICKLY.

AT THE END OF THE HALLS THERE WERE FIRE ALARM BOXES ON THE WALL. THEY WERE BEING SET OFF, WHICH RESULTED IN THE CUSTODIAN AND THE ADMINISTRATION MEETING TO SOLVE THIS PROBLEM. THE PLAN WAS TO SET A TRAP BY COATING THE HANDLES WITH A GOOEY, STICKY SUBSTANCE. THE ALARM PULLER WOULD NOT BE ABLE TO WASH THIS STUFF OFF WITH WATER. SOME DAYS LATER THE FIRE ALARM WAS SET OFF. THE STAFF WENT TO THE FLOOR OF THE ACTIVATED ALARM BOX. WHEN THEY APPROACHED THE FIRE ALARM BOX, THEY SAW A PLASTIC SUPERMARKET BAG HANGING ON THE HANDLE. TWENTY YEARS OF COLLEGE EDUCATION OUT THUNK BY A COUPLE OF JUNIOR HIGH SCHOOL KIDS.

THERE WAS A STAIRCASE AT THE FAR END OF THE BUILDING SOMETIMES CALLED THE BACK STAIRCASE. I OPENED THE DOOR TO GO DOWN THOSE STAIRS AND SAW FRANKIE AGAINST THE WALL WITH A GIRL AGAINST FRANKIE. SHE WAS WEARING A TAN JACKET WITH BIG RED LETTERS ON THE BACK THAT SPELLED NORMA. I TOOK OUT MY HARMONICA AND STARTED PLAYING "LOVE IS A MANY SPLENDERED THING". THEY LEFT THE SCENE AND I CONTINUED DOWN THE STAIRCASE. THIS WAS ONE MORE REASON TO MEET WITH NORMA'S MOM. WHEN WE MET, MOM KEPT REPEATING, "IT WASN'T NORMA, NORMA GAVE HER JACKET TO ANOTHER GIRL, ANOTHER GIRL WAS WEARING NORMA'S JACKET". LUCKY FRANKIE, MAYBE HE HAD TWO GIRLS ON THE BACK STAIRCASE.

SOME YEARS LATER I SAW FRANKIE IN FRONT OF THE SCHOOL. HE TOLD ME HE JUST HAD A FAKE WEDDING. HE SAID A LAWYER SETS UP THE MARRIAGE SO THE GIRL FROM ANOTHER COUNTRY CAN BECOME A CITIZEN. THEY ARE COACHED TO ANSWER ALL THE QUESTIONS. THEY ARE NEVER ALONE TOGETHER. FRANKIE GETS $500 UP FRONT AND ANOTHER $1,000 AFTER THE MARRIAGE IS COMPLETED. FRANKIE SAID THAT HE STILL HASN'T GOTTEN PAID THE $1,000 FOR HIS LAST WEDDING.

DEAN SAM HAD HIS SIDEKICK DEPUTIES, SLIM, RED, TONY, RAY, EVEN WILDBOY. THEY WOULD GO ON PATROL OR BE DISPATCHED WHERE NEEDED. THEY MIGHT BE EQUIPED WITH WALKIE TALKIES AND EVEN USE SOME WALKIE TALKIE CODES AND LANGUAGE. WHILE ON PATROL RAY WAS ALERTED TO GO TO THE BACK OF THE AUDITORIUM. HE OBSERVED TWO STUDENTS BEHIND THE CURTAIN VERY MUCH TOGETHER. RAY PROMPTLY USED HIS WALKIE TALKIE TO REPORT IT TO DEAN SAM. SOME TIME AFTER I ASKED RAY WHAT WAS THE CODE HE USED? HIS ANSWER TO ME WAS NOT THE CODE.

DURING A MONTHLY TEACHER CONFERENCE, THE PRINCIPAL REQUESTED THAT TEACHERS SHOULD BE IN THE HALL DURING PASSING. SO, WHEN THE STUDENTS WENT FROM CLASS TO CLASS, THERE WOULD BE SUPERVISION IN THE HALLS. THE NEXT DAY, AFTER THE PASSING, THE NEIGHBORHOOD CITY COUNCILMAN, MR. O, CAME INTO THE SCHOOL AND WENT RIGHT TO THE MAIN OFFICE HOLDING A TEXTBOOK THAT WAS JUST THROWN OUT A 4TH FLOOR WINDOW. THE NEXT DAY THERE WAS A SHORT MEETING ASKING THE TEACHERS TO HAVE ONE FOOT IN THE HALL AND ONE FOOT IN THE ROOM.

## THE BUMS===*TRYING TO REMEMBER THEM ALL*

NO FULL NAMES TO PROTECT THE GUILTY.

THE GUYS THAT FLOCKED TO THE BUMS ROOM REPRESENTED THE STREETS OF BROOKLYN. THESE WERE GUYS THAT PLAYED STICKBALL ON THE STREETS AND SOFTBALL IN THE SCHOOLYARDS. MOST OF THESE GUYS DID NOT GROW UP PLAYING TENNIS OR SWINGING ON A GOLF COURSE. THE TEACHERS IN THE BUMS ROOM COULD BE DESCRIBED AS A BUNCH OF GUYS HANGING OUT ON A BROOKLYN STREET CORNER. THE ONES THAT WERE NOT STREET CORNER GUYS GROWING UP, STAYED IN THE BUMS ROOM BECAUSE THEY PROBABLY WOULD HAVE LIKED THE SOCIAL SETTING OF THE BROOKLYN STREETS. SOME OF THE ORIGINAL BUMS DID GROW UP ON THE STREETS OF WILLIAMSBURG. WHEN I WENT TO ELEMENTARY SCHOOL IN THE BURG, THE INCOME LEVEL WAS BASICALLY FROM MIDDLE LOW INCOME TO LOW, LOW INCOME.

BACK THEN THERE WERE NO SUPERMARKETS IN WILLIAMSBURG, JUST MOM AND POP STORES. MANY FAMILIES THAT LIVED ON MY BLOCK HAD A CREDIT PAGE AT THE GROCERY STORE NEAR THE CORNER OF THE BLOCK. PEOPLE WOULD BUY FOUR SLICES OF BREAD FROM A LOAF SO SANDWICHES COULD BE MADE FOR THE KIDS' LUNCH. STORES SOLD THREE CIGARETTES FROM THE PACK, CALLING THEM LOOSIES. LOTS OF HAND ME DOWN CLOTHES AND BORROWING A BASEBALL GLOVE FROM A FRIEND WHEN YOU WANTED TO PLAY IN A GAME. THERE WERE NO UNIFORMS, YOU WERE HAPPY TO HAVE SNEAKERS WITH NO HOLES IN THE SOLES. WHEN THERE WERE HOLES IN THE SOLES, YOU WOULD PUT A PIECE OF CARDBOARD INTO YOUR SNEAKER.

THERE WERE ABOUT THIRTY ORIGINAL BUMS MOST OF THEM WERE FROM BROOKLYN. THERE WERE SOME THAT GREW UP IN WILLIAMSBURG AND WENT TO SCHOOLS IN THE BURG. EVERY NEW SCHOOL YEAR THERE WERE OTHER TEACHERS WHO ENJOYED THE BUMS ROOM AND HAD THE QUALIFICATIONS FOR BUMDOM. AS TEACHERS WANDERED AWAY FROM JUNIOR HIGH SCHOOL 50 OTHERS TOOK THEIR PLACE IN THE BUMS CLUB. IN THIS BOOK THERE ARE MANY BUMS CLUB MEMBERS REMEMBERED. THERE IS SOMETHING WRITTEN ABOUT A BUNCH OF THEM. A NUMBER OF TEACHERS THAT WERE BUMS ROOM VISITORS GET HONORABLE MENTION.

MR. ARTIE 1(SHOESHINES IN HIS CLASSROOM, PLAYED ACCORDIAN IN THE TEACHER TALENT SHOW)==MR. ARTIE 2(JUST A NICE GUY, WONDERFUL WELLSIANA SUPERVISOR, GOOD THIRD BASE MAN)==MR. ARMANDO(ALWAYS HAPPY, HAD GOOD RELATIONS WITH THE COMMUNITY, BASKETBALL)==MR. AL 1(INSURANCE SALESMAN, TAUGHT HEBREW A FEW MONTHS ONLY KNOWING ONE WORD, SHOLOM)==MR. AL 3(COMB WITH TOILET PAPER INSTUMENTALS, TABLE DRUMMER)==MR. AL 2(BUMS MOST SERIOUS BUMS PRESIDENT, A CLOSET FOR LEARNING, ANOTHER GREAT TEACHER)==MR. ARTIE 3(REPRESENTED THE BUMS AT ANOTHER SCHOOL, BASKETBALL)==MR. BEN 2(A HUMOROUS INTELLECTUAL, A LOYAL BUM)==BOSS GENE(TOOK CHARGE OF MANY EVENTS, COFFEE CLUB LEADER)==MR. WILLIAM(DISTRICT SUPT. ASKED TO JOIN THE BUMS CLUB)==MR. BARRY(FROM TEACHER TO LAWYER)==ASSISTANTANT PRINCIPAL BERNIE(NOSE AND TOES, TEACHER SUPPORTER, HAD OUR BACK, STUDENT FAVORITE)==MR. BEN 1(BIGGER THAN LIFE, BUMS ROOM INTELLECTUAL, PUT ASSISTANT PRINCIPAL MISS AUDREY. OVER HIS

SHOULDER)== HANDYMAN DAVE{PUT LIGHT IN OUR CLASSROOMS) ==MR. DON(SUPPLIED BUMS ROOM PARTIES WITH HOMEMADE VINO, BECAME A PRINCIPAL)==MR. DICK(THE WHITE SHADOW, NOT THE USUAL MUSIC TEACHER)==DEAN SAM(HE WAS A STORY BOOK BY HIMSELF, ABDUCTED AND HELD THE ROBBER HOSTAGE IN HIS BASEMENT, THE STORY WAS CONFIRMED)== PRINCIPAL FRANK(AS SOON AS HE TOOK THE PRINCIPALSHIP HE WAS READY FOR BUMDOM)==MR. FRANK 1{HAD A LICENSE TO CARRY}==MR. GIL(ORIGINAL BUM LEFT US EARLY TOWARD AN ADMINISTRATIVE CAREER}==MR. GENE(OUR TAX ADVISOR, SORT OF SERIOUS, SOFTBALL PLAYER)==MR. GERRY{COLLEGE CENTERFIELDER, LIKED THE TABLECLOTH EVENT)==MR. JERRY(PRANKIST, ENJOYED THE BUMS ROOM, STIRRED UP CONVERSATION)==MR. JOE 1(OUR CHAPTER CHAIRMAN, DIDN'T LIKE TO HEAR THE PM DISMISSAL BELL)==MR. JEFF 1(PRANKERIST, TRIP PARTNER OF THE TRIP KING, STUDENTS LOVED HIM)==MR. JOHN(PRANKPRO, BUMS' LICENSED STOCKBROKER)==MR. JEFF 2(HAD JOB AT THE RACETRACK, RACED FAR TO SUFFOLK COUNTY)==MR. LEONARD(40 YEARS AT J.H.S. 50, TEACHER TALENT SHOW LEADER)==MR. LENNY 1(MORNING SCRATCH OFF FUN, THE SLEEPING CIGAR)==MR. LESTER{INVITED US TO THE SCHAEFER HOUSE}==MR. MIKE 1(SOLD STOCKS AND BELT BUCKLES IN BUMS ROOM)==MR. MARIO(DISTRICT UNION REP, BROUGHT THE TEACHERS BACK)==MR. MARK(MEDICAL LAB SPECIALIST, TOOK BLOOD IN THE CORNER OF THE BUMS ROOM)==MISS MARIE(OUR ONLY FEMALE MEMBER, SHE CRIED WHEN THE VOTE WAS UNANIMOUS)==MR. MEL(ORDERED THE GOLD BUM PINS, BASKETBALL IN THE MORNING, WAS A BUMS PRESIDENT)==MR. MARTY 1{TAUGHT IN=SERVICE COURSES, BASKETBALL IN THE MORNING}==MR.

MARV(BETTING ODDS EXPERT, SUPERVISED THE AVOID THE ASSISTANT PRINCIPAL GETTING THE SNACKS GAME)==MR. NAT(DEAN, LUNCHROOM COORDINATOR, REMEMBERED FOR BANGING HIS WOOD 2 BY 4 ON THE TABLE TO CONTROL NOISE IN CAFETERIA)==MR. PETE 1((LIKED TO DECORATE THE BUMS ROOM WALLS WITH HUMOR, WAS A BUMS PRESIDENT)==MR. PETE 2(CAME TO SCHOOL WITH A MOTORCYCLE, ASKED MR. LENNY 2 IF HE EVER TURNS THE PAGE?)==MR. ROBERT 1( WELL KNOWN MARSHALL ARTS INSTRUCTOR, TRIED TEACHING A MEMORY IMPROVEMENT CLASS BUT FORGOT TO SHOW UP FOR THE FIRST SESSION)==MR. ROBERT 2(THE BUMS WILLIAMSBURG HISTORIAN)==MR. STANLEY(BOOK CONTRIBUTOR, KNOWN FOR HIS BATTLE CRIES WHEN HEADING OUT OF THE BUMS ROOM TO TEACH)== DR. SAM(TOOK SHORT COURSE TO BE A DOCTOR, TEACHER TALENT SHOW SONG AND DANCEMAN)==MR. SAM 1 (THE DENTIST PULLED THE WRONG TOOTH, THIS MIGHT HAVE SUMMARIZED HIS EVERYDAY LUCK)==MR. SAM 2(CRAFTSMAN EXTROARDINAIRE, DEAN, SWIMMING INSTRUCTOR)==MR. SID 2(WELL READ, COULD DISCUSS WITH AUTHORITY)==MR. S.(AUTHORED REQUEST FORMS,BOOK CONTRIBUTOR)==MR. STEVE(HIGH VOLUME, BASKETBALL, ORIGINAL IN EVERY WAY)== MR. VINNY(PRANKOLOGIST, FIRST BUMS PRESIDENT, BUMS ROOM STIMULATOR)==MR. WARREN(PRANKERER, MULTI=CLASS TRIP COORDINATOR, HUMORIST, THE BELT PARKWAY, THE WHITE SHADOW).

OVER THE YEARS MANY OF THE ORIGINAL BUMS LEFT JUNIOR HIGH SCHOOL 50 FOR VARIOUS REASONS. CHANGING SCHOOLS TO BE CLOSER TO HOME, CHANGING PROFESSIONS LIKE COMPUTER PROGRAMMER, LAWYER, NURSE. MOVING TO

ASSISTANT PRINCIPAL IN ANOTHER SCHOOL OR GUIDANCE COUNSELOR IN ANOTHER AREA. THE YEAR 1995, THERE WAS A RETIREMENT INCENTIVE RESULTING IN A NUMBER OF BUMS PACKING IT IN. MANY OF THESE TEACHERS HAD THIRTY OR MORE YEARS IN THE SYSTEM. AS BUMS LEFT, IN THEIR PLACE WERE NEW TEACHERS THAT ENJOYED THE ATMOSPHERE OF THE BUMS ROOM. THERE WAS PLENTY FOR THEM TO LEARN IF THEY HAD THE THOUGHT OF REMAINING IN THE TEACHING PROFESSION. THE NEW TEACHERS COULD BE GIVEN IDEAS FOR KEEPING DISCIPLINE, OR PICKUP IDEAS FOR TEACHING PROCEDURES OR WAYS TO INCREASE THEIR SALARIES. THE BUMS WERE AVAILABLE FOR EACH OTHER AND ESPECIALLY FOR THE NEW TEACHERS. MOST OF THE NEW TEACHERS WERE NOT JUST OUT OF COLLEGE, THEY HAD JOBS BEFORE TRYING THE TEACHING PROFESSION. THE STARTING SALARY FOR NEW TEACHERS WAS A STRUGGLE FOR THEM. EDUCATION REQUIREMENT COSTS, LIVING COSTS AND THE REST HAD SOME TEACHERS BORROWING MONEY TO EAT AT THE END OF THE PAY PERIOD.

HERE ARE SOME OF THE NEWER TEACHERS THAT WOULD VISIT OR HANGOUT IN THE BUMS ROOM. A TERRIFIC GROUP OF GUYS, MOST SINGLE AND NOT RIGHT OUT OF COLLEGE.

MR. MIKE 2(WAS A ROOFER, STILL DID ROOFING ON HIS DAYS OFF}== MR. TIM(WORKED WITH AN ELECTRICAL CONTRACTOR)==MR. MARTY 2(STARTED LEARNING TO PLAY THE HARMONICA)==MR. PETE 3(WORKED AS A CARPENTER. HE DID WORK FOR SOME TEACHERS. SOME THOUGHT TEACHING WAS THE RIGHT PLACE FOR HIM)==MR. OSVALDO(ESL TEACHING PROGRAM, LEARNED MUCHO ENGLISH IN

THE BUMS ROOM)==MR. GUS(ESL TEACHER, ANSWERED WITH THE WORD, YES, TO EVERY QUESTION)==MR. HENRY(HE JUDGED OUR RELIGIOUS LEVEL, PRAYED FOR THE BUMS EVERYDAY)==MR. ED(EXTRA STRONG, LIKED TO LIFT PEOPLE WHILE THEY SAT ON A CHAIR)==MR. AL 4(MIDWEST COLLEGE FOOTBALL RUNNING BACK, TRYING TO ADJUST TO JUNIOR HIGH SCHOOL 50)==MR. FRANK 2(ONE SERIOUS GUY, PURSUED A NURSING CAREER)==MR. JAMES(LANDED THE JOB OF ART TEACHER)== MR. JAIME( AN IVY LEAGUE TYPE GUY)

IF YOU WANTED TO DISPLAY YOUR INTELLECTUAL PROWESS, THE BUMS ROOM WAS NOT THE PLACE. THE BUMS ROOM WAS A HAVEN FOR CLUBROOM ANTICS, HUMOR AND UNCONVENTIONAL CHARACTERS. THE ORIGINAL BUMS WERE A COMPLETELY DIFFERENT BREED THAN THE NEWER GUYS. THE ORIGINAL BUMS CAME WITH A TEACHING LICENSE, MANY OF THE NEW TEACHERS HAD TO TAKE EDUCATION COURSES TO VALIDATE THE LICENSE. THE ORIGINAL BUMS WERE HIRED BY THE CENTRAL BOARD OF EDUCATION. WHEN COMMUNITY CONTROL WAS PUT INTO PLACE, THE NEWER TEACHERS COULD BE HIRED TO FILL POSITIONS BY THE COMMUNITY DISTRICT OFFICE AND THEN TAKE THE COURSES TO FULFILL THE NECESSARY REQUIREMENTS. THE NEWER BUMS GAVE A NEW FLAVOR TO THE BUMS ROOM. MANY OF THE ORIGINAL BUMS WERE MARRIED WITH CHILDREN, THE NEW BUMS WERE MOSTLY SINGLE IN A COMPLETELY DIFFERENT SPACE. TWO DIFFERENT GROUPS OF TEACHERS, ONE THAT AT ONE TIME WORE SPORT COATS AND TIES AND THE NEW GROUP THAT POSSIBLY DIDN'T OWN A TIE. ONE VERY VISIBLE DIFFERENCE BETWEEN THE TWO GROUPS WAS ONE GROUP WAS MULTI TATTOOED WHILE IT

WOULD BE HARD TO FIND ONE TATTOO ON THE ORIGINAL BUMS. THESE TATTOOED GUYS ENJOYED THE LOOSENESS OF THE BUMS ROOM AND EXHIBITED QUALITIES FOR BUMDOM.

**THE BUMS ROOM HAD IT ALL!**

MR. S. ALWAYS JOKED "ANYTHING YOU WANTED COULD BE GOTTEN IN THE BUMS ROOM. THE TEACHERS IN THE BUMS ROOM HAD A WIDE RANGE OF SECOND JOBS AND INTERESTS. WHEN YOU WERE IN THE BUMS ROOM YOU HEARD INFORMATION AND ADVICE FLOW FREELY. ALL TOPICS AND ISSUES WERE PUT FORTH WITH ENTHUSIASM. ONE BUM WAS EMPHATIC THAT YOU ENHANCE THE MEAL WITH THE COLOR OF SODA CONSUMED WITH THE MEAL. HE SAID RED SODA SHOULD PARTNER WITH A MEAT MEAL WHILE LIGHT SODA GOES BEST WITH FISH. THIS GUY WOULD EAT PUTTING THE FORK TO HIS MOUTH UPSIDE DOWN. IN THE BUMS ROOM YOU DIDN'T ALWAYS GET QUALITY INFORMATION. THE BEST COMMENTS CAME FROM THE DEVIL'S ADVOCATES, THE VOICES OF DOOM, AND THE CONTRARIAN CONTINGENT.

MR. S. WOULD GO THROUGH A WHOLE LIST OF SERVICES THAT COULD BE DELIVERED BY THE BUMS CLUB MEMBERS AND THE BUMS ROOM VISITORS. HE DID THIS WITH HIS USUAL DRY HUMOR. IF YOU NEEDED INSURANCE, MR. AL 1 WAS AN INSURANCE SALESMAN AND DID HAVE CLIENTS IN THE BUMS ROOM. MR. GENE DID THE TAX RETURNS FOR MR. S AND SOME OTHER GUYS IN THE BUMS ROOM. IF YOU WANTED KARATE LESSONS, THEY WERE GIVEN MORNINGS IN THE GYM BY MR. ROBERT 1. MR. MARK WORKED IN A MEDICAL LAB, AND ACTUALLY TOOK BLOOD FROM MR. STANLEY IN THE CORNER OF THE BUMS ROOM. MR. JOHN AND MR. MIKE 1 WERE LICENSED STOCKBROKERS. THEY HAD CUSTOMERS FOR THAT THREE DOLLAR HEALTH AND BEAUTY STOCK TAUTED BY THEM IN THE BUMS ROOM. SHOP TEACHERS DID WORK AT MANY TEACHERS' HOMES

INCLUDING MANY BUMS AND THE PRINCIPAL. CARPENTRY, PLUMBING, AND ELECTRICAL, ALL SERVICES WERE AVAILABLE RIGHT FROM THE BUMS ROOM.

LIKE IN THE REAL WORLD THERE WERE MANY HAPPY RESULTS, WHILE THERE WERE BUSINESS DEALINGS THAT DID NOT GO WELL. THIS GAVE THE CONTRARIANS PLENTY OF MATERIAL AND AMMUNITION. IN THE BUMS ROOM YOU WOULD HEAR IF YOU NEEDED CARPENTRY WORK DONE IN YOUR HOUSE, WHY WOULD YOU HIRE SOMEONE THAT SPENDS HIS WORK WEEK SHOWING KIDS HOW TO SAND A PIECE OF WOOD. YOU WOULD HEAR, WHY WOULD YOU CONSIDER INVESTING YOUR MONEY WITH SOMEONE THAT'S IN A CLASSROOM ALL DAY WITH THIRTY KIDS? YOU MIGHT DO BETTER WITH THE KIDS PICKING THE STOCKS. THE BUMS ROOM WAS FULL OF RIDICULE. IN ANY EVENT, MR. S. WAS CORRECT, THERE WERE MANY SERVICES AVAILABLE IN THAT ROOM. THERE WAS A LOCKSMITH AND KEY MAKER AS WELL AS EXPERTS IN SPORTS BETTING. MR. JERRY WAS WITH A RECORD COMPANY, HIS RECORD PLAYED ON THE RADIO AND HE APPEARED ON WCBS=FM RADIO. MR. ROBERT 1. APPEARED IN VARIOUS MARSHALL ARTS MAGAZINES AND TAUGHT IT FOR MANY YEARS. MR. BEN 1 WAS A CHESS EXPERT SPENDING TIME TEACHING STUDENTS TO PLAY CHESS. MR. SID 2 HAD A WRITING TALENT, HE HELPED STUDENTS WRITE COLLEGE ADMISSION ESSAYS OR JOB APPLICATIONS. A NUMBER OF BUMS WERE MILITARY VETERANS WHICH ENABLED THEM TO GET A FREE COLLEGE EDUCATION AND SPEAK ABOUT MILITARY PROCEDURES. YOU WOULD HEAR SOME INTERESTING STORIES FROM ALL OF THEM. MR. PETE 1 WAS A WEIGHTLIFTER, MR. STEVE PLAYED COLLEGE FOOTBALL, BOTH WERE PRETTY

VOCAL WHEN THE CONVERSATION IN THE BUMS ROOM WAS SPORTS. MR. MIKE 2 COULD ADVISE ON REPAIRING A ROOF.

THE BUMS ROOM WAS A UNIQUE PLACE WITH TEACHERS HAVING VARIOUS INTERESTS READY TO KEEP THE CONVERSATIONS GOING. MR. STANLEY WAS A PHOTOGRAPHER WHO TAUGHT PHOTOGRAPHY IN A CUMMUNITY COLLEGE. MR. S. WOULD POINT OUT THE MANY VISITORS TO THE BUMS ROOM THAT PERFORMED SERVICES THAT BUMS COULD ENJOY. MR. LENNY 2 WAS A MASSAGE THERAPIST, MR. JEFF 2 COULD IMPROVE YOUR SEATING AT THE RACETRACK AND MR. ARTIE 2, WHO WORKED AFTER SCHOOL AT A SWEATER FACTORY, OFFERED SWEATERS AT DISCOUNT PRICES. THERE WERE A NUMBER OF LAWYERS AND LAW SCHOOL STUDENTS THAT LOOKED TO RELAX IN THE BUMS ROOM. THE LAWYERS DID GET SOME CLIENT WORK FROM THE BUMS ROOM. THE LAW STUDENTS WERE USUALLY STUDYING SOMEWHERE IN THE SCHOOL ON THEIR FREE TIME. THERE WAS A RABBI=TEACHER THAT CAME INTO THE BUMS ROOM. OF COURSE, RABBI MEANS TEACHER. ANYWAY, RABBI MARVIN ONCE HELPED MR. JERRY WITH A PASSOVER COOKING BLENDER QUESTION. MR. JERRY WAS WONDERING IF THERE IS A PROCESS THAT COULD MAKE THE BLENDER THAT IS USED ALL YEAR USABLE FOR THE PASSOVER HOLIDAY. MR. JERRY WAS EXPECTING EITHER NO OR A COMPLICATED ANSWER. RABBI MARVIN ANSWERED, "DO YOU HAVE HOT WATER?" THIS ISSUE WAS MADE EASY AND UNCOMPLICATED IN THE BUMS ROOM.

MR. S. IN HIS HUMOROUS WAY COULD RATTLE OFF A DOZEN SERVICES THAT COULD BE GOTTEN IN THE

BUMS ROOM. HE PROBABLY COULD PUT IT INTO RHYME.

IN THE BUMS ROOM YOU CAN MAKE A BET
A FINANCIAL ADVISOR HELPS YOU OUT OF DEBT
THERE'S SOMEONE TO TAKE YOUR BLOOD
A PLUMBER TO STOP THE FLOOD
GET INSURANCE, CAR OR LIFE
BUY A SWEATER FOR YOUR WIFE
A LOCKSMITH TO SECURE YOUR DOOR
A CARPENTER TO INSTALL A FLOOR
PAINTING OR ART FOR YOUR WALL
MR. S. SAYS THE BUMS ROOM HAD IT ALL

## DISTRICT 14 IN THE NEWS

THE COMMUNITY SCHOOL BOARD CONSISTING OF NINE MEMBERS, ELECTS THE DISTRICT SUPERINTENDANT TO OVERSEE THE ELEMENTARY, MIDDLE AND JUNIOR HIGH SCHOOLS, ALL THE SCHOOLS IN THE DISTRICT. THE DISTRICT SUPERINTENDANT IS WELL PAID WITH MUCH RESPECT AND HAS THE INFLUENCE TO HELP PLACE PEOPLE IN VARIOUS JOBS. HAVING A GOOD RELATIONSHIP WITH THE COMMUNITY SCHOOL BOARD MEMBERS HELPS BEING RE=ELECTED TO THE SUPERINTENDANT POSITION. IN DISTRICT 14 MANY OF THE SCHOOL BOARD MEMBERS DID NOT HAVE CHILDREN IN THE PUBLIC SCHOOL SYSTEM. IN FACT, THEY HAD INTEREST IN THE NEIGHBORHOOD RELIGIOUS SCHOOL. LIKE EVERYWHERE IN POLITICS, DOING THINGS FOR THOSE WHOSE VOTES YOU NEED HELPS GET YOU RE=ELECTED. HERE, THE GOVERNMENT FELT THE "DOING THINGS" FOR THE RELIGIOUS SCHOOL WAS NOT KOSHER.

IN THE COMPLEX WORLD OF GOVERNMENT AND POLITICS THERE ARE DIFFERENT CATAGORIES OF MONEY. TAX LEVY MONEY IS AVAILABLE FOR THE PUBLIC SCHOOLS AND NOT FOR PRIVATE SCHOOLS. CHAPTER ONE MONEY CAN BE AVAILABLE TO PRIVATE SCHOOLS UNDER CERTAIN CIRCUMSTANCES. HAVING DIFFERENT CATAGORIES AND DEPARTMENTS MAKES IT EASIER TO EMPLOY MORE FRIENDS AND RELATIVES. APPARENTLY, SOME COMMUNITY SCHOOL BOARD MEMBERS ASSOCIATED WITH A PRIVATE SCHOOL MADE A DEAL WITH THE DISTRICT 14 OFFICE TO GET SOME FUNDS TO THE RELIGIOUS SCHOOL. THE WAYS THE MONEY WAS DISTRIBUTED AND THE REASONS FOR WHICH THE MONEY WAS

PAID OUT RESULTED IN AN INVESTIGATION OF DISTRICT 14.
THE NEW YORK TIMES STORY OF MAY 17, 1999, WROTE ABOUT THE DISTRICT 14 SUPERINTENDANT AND THE INVESTIGATION THAT TOOK PLACE. THE STORY DESCRIBED HIM AS A TOUGH IMAGE GUY, SAYING THAT HE POINTED OUT THAT HIS INITIALS SPELLED WAR. IT COMMENTED THAT HE NAMED A SCHOOL, THE JOHN WAYNE SCHOOL, AFTER HIS FAVORITE ACTOR, EVEN THOUGH THE STUDENT BODY WAS LARGELY HISPANIC.

VARIOUS GOVERNMENT AGENCIES GOT INVOLVED IN THE INVESTIGATION. THE U. S. ATTORNEY FOR THE EASTERN DISTRICT OF N.Y., INVESTIGATED AND ASSEMBLED EVIDENCE WHICH LED TO GUILTY PLEAS AND CONVICTIONS. ED STANCIK, SPECIAL COMMISSIONER OF INVESTIGATION FOR THE NEW YORK CITY SCHOOL DISTRICT, NOTIFIED CHANCELLOR RUDOLPH CREW OF HIS FINDINGS AND RELATED SUGGESTIONS. THE INVESTIGATION INVOLVED AND DISCOVERED TAXPAYER DOLLARS PAYING SALARIES AND BENEFITS TO NO=SHOW EMPLOYEES AT THE RELIGIOUS SCHOOL. THESE ALLEGATIONS INVOVLED THE DISTRICT SUPERINTENDANT AND A NUMBER OF PEOPLE ASSOCIATED WITH THE RELIGIOUS SCHOOL. IT WAS ALLEDGED THAT THE DISTRICT SUPERINTENDANT SUPPLIED THE FUNDS FOR NO=SHOW EMPLOYEES OVER A NUMBER OF YEARS. THE ED STANCIK INVESTIGATION CONFIRMED THE FINDINGS.

ACCORDING TO THE REPORT THERE WERE DOZENS OF THE NO=SHOW JOBS PAID BY NEW YORK CITY BOARD OF EDUCATION MONEY TO PEOPLE RELATED TO THE RELIGIOUS SCHOOL. IN THE REPORT, THE U.S. ATTORNEY FOR THE EASTERN DISTRICT OF NEW

YORK PROSECUTED AND CONVICTED FOUR CONSPIRATORS WITH GUILTY PLEAS, FOR MONEY ILLEGALLY OBTAINED FROM THE BOARD OF EDUCATION. IT WAS REPORTED THAT THIS CONSPIRACY WENT FROM THE 1970'S TO 1994 WITH THE BOARD OF EDUCATION PAYING ABOUT $4.3 MILLION IN SALARIES TO ABOUT EIGHTY PEOPLE. THE BOARD OF EDUCATION ALSO PAID PEOPLE ABOUT $1.9 MILLION IN BENEFITS. THE ARRANGEMENT WAS THE SALARIES WOULD BE KICKED BACK TO THE RELIGIOUS SCHOOL WHILE THE NO=SHOW EMPLOYEES WERE HAPPY TO GET HEALTH BENEFITS.

APPARENTLY, THIS WAS NOT A SIMPLE OPERATION. EVERY TWO WEEKS THE SIGNED TIME SHEETS OF THE NO=SHOW EMPLOYEES WOULD BE DELIVERED TO THE DISTRICT OFFICE TO BE PROCESSED. ONE REPORT TALKS ABOUT SECURITY GUARDS BEING EMPLOYED, PAID WITH CHAPTER ONE MONEY, WHICH IS MONEY ONLY TO BE USED FOR EDUCATIONAL PROGRAMS. ALSO 1991 RECORDS SHOWED THE RELIGIOUS SCHOOL HAD THIRTY ONE SCHOOL GUARDS IN TAX LEVY POSITIONS, ALTHOUGH TAX LEVY FUNDS ARE NOT FOR PRIVATE SCHOOLS.

THE REPORT WRITES THAT THE DISTRICT 14 OFFICE DID THE ADMINISTRATIVE TASKS LIKE TIMESHEETS, PAYROLL RECORDS AND DRIVING NO=SHOW PROSPECTIVES TO BE FINGERPRINTED AT THE BOARD OF EDUCATION. THE NO=SHOW SCHEME DEALT WITH SCHOOL FUNDING PROCEDURES. TAX LEVY DOLLARS SHOULD NOT BE USED FOR CHILDREN IN PRIVATE OR RELIGIOUS SCHOOLS. FEDERAL CHAPTER ONE MONEY MAY BE USED IF THE SCHOOL MEETS THE REQUIREMENTS FOR THE PROGRAM. IT

WAS REPORTED THAT THE BOARD OF EDUCATION FUNDS WERE SPENT IMPROPERLY.

THE VACATION DAY CAMP WAS A WONDERFUL SUMMER PROGRAM IN DISTRICT 14. EACH VACATION DAY CAMP PROGRAM COULD HAVE A STAFF OF TEN. FIVE TEACHERS, AIDES, SECURITY AND MAYBE LUNCH WORKERS. THE RELIGIOUS SCHOOL VACATION DAY CAMP PROGRAM SOMETIMES REACHED FIFTY EMPLOYEES. IN REALITY THERE WAS NO VACATION DAY CAMP AT THE RELIGIOUS SCHOOL. THE TIME SHEETS WERE PROVIDED POST DATED, NO=SHOWS WERE PAID FOR THE SUMMER.

THE SUMMER SCAM WENT ON FROM 1982 TO 1992, THE YEAR WHEN THE ED STANCYK INVESTIGATION STARTED. THE REPORT OF THE INVESTIGATION IN THIS BOOK IS BASICALLY FROM THE INVESTIGATIONS OF THE U.S. ATTORNEY FOR THE EASTERN DISTRICT OF NEW YORK AND ED STANCYK, SPECIAL COMMISSIONER OF INVESTIGATION FOR THE NEW YORK CITY SCHOOL DISTRICT.
ED STANCYK'S REPORT TO CHANCELOR RUDOLPH CREW SUGGESTED THERE WERE CHILDREN OF THE LOCAL SCHOOL BOARD MEMBERS THAT WERE NO=SHOW EMPLOYEES.

THE REPORT SUGGESTED THAT THE THREE COMMUNITY SCHOOL BOARD MEMBERS BE REMOVED FROM THE BOARD. THE ARTICLE, "IN SCHOOL DISTRICT, CORRUPTION FED BY ETHIC DIVISION" APPEARED IN THE NEW YORK TIMES MAY 17, 1999. IT CONCLUDED THERE WERE FIFTY= NINE NO SHOW JOBS, $6 MILLION PAID OUT OVER THE TWENTY YEARS SCHEME TO GET THE SUPPORT OF THE THREE SCHOOL BOARD MEMBERS, WHO WERE ASSOCIATED WITH THE RELIGIOUS SCHOOL.

THE TWO SCHOOL DISTRICT 14 SUPERINTENDANTS INVOLVED ARE NO LONGER WITH US. MR. WILLIAM AND MR. MARIO=== R.I.P.

## BUMS ARE REMEMBERED===*TAKE A BOW*

NO FULL NAMES TO PROTECT THE GUILTY.

JOHN D. WELLS J.H.S. 50 IS A GROUP SITE SET UP ON FACEBOOK. JOHN D. WELLS IS THE SCHOOL'S NAME AND MANY STUDENTS REFER TO THE SCHOOL BY THIS NAME. ON THIS SITE THERE ARE STUDENTS WRITING THEIR IDEAS, THOUGHTS AND RESPONSES TO OTHER STUDENTS. AFTER VIEWING THIS SITE IT WAS A HOME RUN FOR ME TO INCLUDE THE THOUGHTS OF PAST STUDENTS IN THE "THE BUMS CLUB" BOOK. QUESTIONS WERE POSTED TO THE JUNIOR HIGH SCHOOL 50 STUDENTS THAT ATTENDED JUNIOR HIGH SCHOOL 50 DURING THE THIRTY YEARS OF THE BUMS CLUB. THIS RESULTED IN MANY ENJOYABLE AND INTERESTING RESPONSES.

THERE WERE POSTS FROM STUDENTS AND TEACHERS THAT WERE WELL RECEIVED. MR. JERRY POSTED "ANY J.H.S. 50 STUDENTS AT J.H.S. 50 IN THE 1960'S, 1970'S OR 1980'S". THIS POST RECEIVED 164 RESPONSES. THE POST "J.H.S. 50 1970 TO 1990 YOUR SCIENCE TEACHERS???" RECEIVED 35 ANSWERS. THE POST "STUDENTS FROM 1965 TO 1995, WHO WAS YOUR FUNNIEST TEACHER?" GOT 26 ANSWERS. A GREAT POST WAS "YOUR FAVORITE LUNCHROOM MEAL??" IT GOT 42 DELICIOUS RESPONSES.

MANY OF THE RESPONSES INCLUDED BEAUTIFUL FEELINGS, THOUGHTS AND MEMORIES OF THE SCHOOL AND BUMS CLUB MEMBERS. READING ABOUT THEIR JUNIOR HIGH SCHOOL 50 EXPERIENCES WAS HEARTWARMING. SEEING HOW THESE STUDENTS REMEMBERED BOTH EDUCATIONAL AND HUMOROUS SITUATIONS MADE ME UNDERSTAND THAT THEY HAD A PLEASANT EXPERIENCE DURING THEIR YEARS AT

JOHN D. WELLS 50. WHEN WRITING THE STUDENT RESPONSES THERE WILL NOT BE FULL NAMES, ONLY FIRST NAMES EVEN THOUGH, WHO'S GOING TO READ THIS ANYWAY? TO THE POST ABOUT YOUR FAVORITE SCIENCE TEACHER, THERE WERE SOME WONDERFUL COMMENTS. COLLEEN ANSWERED MR. MIKE 1 AND ADDED THAT SHE HAD GREAT MEMORIES OF YOU ALL. STUDENT S.D. WROTE, MR GEORGE ALWAYS WORE A BOW TIE AND SUIT. SHE ADDED, THE TEACHERS ALL WORE SUITS IN THE DAY, WITH TIES. I BELIEVE HE NEVER LAUGHED. IT WAS THE ONLY CLASS WITH INKWELL DESKS. D.M. WROTE, I HAVE FOND MEMORIES OF MR. GEORGE HE AWARDED ME WITH THE SCIENCE MEDAL. SANDRA WROTE, SHE REMEMBERS MR. GEORGE AND THE PERIODIC TABLE.

THERE WAS A DECISION THAT ALL THE DESKS AND SEATS THAT WERE ATTACHED TO THE FLOOR BE REPLACED BY FREE STANDING TABLES AND CHAIRS. THIS WAS NOT WANTED BY MR. GEORGE HE GOT TO KEEP HIS OLD, FASTENED TO THE FLOOR INKWELL DESKS AND SEATS. OTHER FAVORITE BUM SCIENCE TEACHERS MENTIONED WERE MR. TIM, AND MR. MARK.

THE RESPONSES TO THE FUNNIEST TEACHER POST DID HAVE SOME SPECIAL REPLIES. WHEN MR. AL 2 WOULD GO INTO HIS STORAGE ROOM THE WORLD WOULD FOLLOW HIM OUT, EXCELLENT EDUCATOR. ERVING WROTE, THE WORLD WAS ON THE OTHER SIDE OF THAT CLOSET DOOR. SARITA SAID, HE WAS SO QUIRKY. HIS QUIRKY CLOSET MADE SOCIAL STUDIES MORE INTERESTING AND FUN. ELIUT LIKED MR. STUART, IT WAS FUN WHEN HIS EXPERIMENTS IN CLASS NEVER WORKED.

THERE WAS A LIST OF 25 FUNNY TEACHERS. MR. VINNY. WAS ON TOP OF THE LIST. DAVID SAID, MR. VINNY HANDS DOWN. HILLARY AND LILLIAN BOTH RESPONDED MR. VINNY AND MR. HARVEY, THESE WERE THE BEST. A STUDENT WROTE, I WILL NEVER FORGET MR. VINNY. WHEN WE WERE TALKING ABOUT ACNE AND A STUDENT ASKED IF PREPARATION H WAS GOOD FOR PIMPLES AND MR. VINNY AND THE ENTIRE CLASS BROKE UP IN LAUGHTER, BUT THE KID WAS PUZZLED WHY WE WERE LAUGHING. THEN MR. VINNY SAID PREPARATION PH IS FOR PIMPLES, PREPARATION H IS FOR YOUR CULO. WE LOST IT, MR. VINNY SAID CULO IN CLASS.

OTHER TEACHERS WERE REMEMBERED AS FUNNY TEACHERS. JEANNETTE RESPONDED, "I HAVE TO SAY MR. MIKE 2 AND THAT WHOLE GANG". STUDENT MIRIAM RESPONDED THAT SHE REMEMBERED MR. NAT, DEAN SAM, AND MR. ROBERT 1, THEN ADDED SHE ENJOYED HER 3 YEARS AT J.H.S. 50. JOHN DRY WELLS.

FROM THE REPLIES TO THE POSTS, THE APPRECIATION FOR THE SCHOOL AND THE TEACHERS WAS QUITE APPARENT.

THE POST "ANY J.H.S. 50 STUDENTS AT J.H.S. 50 IN THE 1960, 1970, 1980's ???" AMASSED 164 RESPONSES AND WAS ANOTHER INFLUENCE FOR WRITING THIS BOOK.

STUDENT TONY WRITES, I REMEMBER HAVING A CRUSH ON THE GIRL WITH THE TWO LONG PIGTAILS. YEP, BUT SHE WAS OUT OF MY CLASS, MIGHT STILL BE. DEBORAH ANSWERED, NO ONE WAS OUT OF YOUR LEAGUE, YOU THE MAN!!!

AMY WROTE, I WAS THERE FOR ONE YEAR. HOWEVER, I ATTENDED THE SUMMER CAMP FOR YEARS AND LOVED IT. SHE IS REFERRING TO THE VACATION DAY CAMP [VDC] PROGRAM. SHE WROTE MR. JERRY YES, I REMEMBER YOU! WE LIVED RIGHT ACROSS FROM J.H.S. 50 AT 182 S. 3$^{RD}$. ST.
EDWIN WROTE YES, HE SAID THAT HE WAS MR. JOHN D. WELLS HIS SENIOR YEAR.
ELIUT WRITES, MY FRIEND AND MENTOR U MADE ME THE MAN I AM TODAY. THANK YOU, MR. JERRY.
ROSE ADDS GREAT TEACHERS TOO. STEVE, I WAS THE G. O. PRESIDENT.
MOST OF THE 164 RESPONSES WERE JUST NAMES, THE YEARS THEY WERE AT THE SCHOOL AND FRIENDLY ACKNOWLEDGEMENTS TO EACH OTHER.

THE QUESTION, "WHO WAS IN CHARGE OF YOUR LUNCHROOM?" GARNERED ONLY 10 ANSWERS. THE ANSWERS INCLUDED MR. SAM 2, MR. VINNY, MR. MARK, MR. NAT WITH HIS 2" X 4" HITTING THE TABLES, TO GET THE ATTENTION OF THE DINERS. A STUDENT FABIOLA, WRITES MR. VINNY WAS THE BEST BUT HE GAVE REFERRAL CARDS THAT MEANT TROUBLE.
RICHARD WROTE JULIA CHILDS. THIS KID WAS ALWAYS FUNNY. THERE WAS HUMOR IN MANY STUDENTS.

YOUR FAVORITE LUNCHROOM MEAL QUESTION BROUGHT BACK MEMORIES OF THE FOODS SERVED WHEN I HAD LUNCHROOM DUTY. THAT DUTY FOR TEACHERS STOPPED WHEN THEY USED AIDES FOR MONITORING THE LUNCHROOM. THE MOST POPULAR FOOD ANSWERS SERVED BY THE STUDENTS WERE SLOPPY JOE, STUFFED FISH SANDWICH, GRILLED CHEESE, FISH STICKS ON FRIDAY, SQUARE PIZZA, HOT DOG WITH SAUERKRAUT, BREADED FRIED CHICKEN,

MEATLOAF, ROUND PEPPERONI PIZZA, BURGERS AND MOZZARELLA STICKS: MANY STUDENTS INCLUDED THE SIDE DISHES, FRIES, MASHED POTATOES, TATOR TOTS, AND PEAS. TWO BIG FAVORITES WERE CHOCOLATE MILK AND SCOOTER PIE. THE LUNCHROOM STAFF WAS WONDERFUL. THE NAMES I REMEMBER ARE MR. WALLS, MISS CARRIE, MR. MARK, MISS REGGIE AND MISS TERESA. THANKS FOR YOUR TERRIFIC COOKING AND SERVICE.
IN THEIR RESPONSES TO THE POSTS THE STUDENTS SHOWED FONDNESS AND APPRECIATION FOR THE MEALS SERVED BY THE LUNCHROOM STAFF.

IT WAS QUITE UPLIFTING READING THE HEARTFELT RESPONSES TO ALL THE FACEBOOK POSTS. HERE ARE SOME MORE OF THE STUDENT'S WRITINGS SHOWING THE RESPECT, GRATITUDE AND AFFECTION THE STUDENTS HAD FOR JUNIOR HIGH SCHOOL 50 AND THEIR TEACHERS.
BROOKLYN WRITES, WHEN I THINK ABOUT THESE YEARS IN COMPARISON TO TODAY, WE WERE SO FORTUNATE, THE GREATEST TEACHERS. WE LEARNED FOREIGN LANGUAGES, WE LEARNED MUSIC, SHOP CLASSES, SEWING, COOKING...ETC! WE DIDN'T REALIZE IT AT THE TIME, BUT WE WERE EXPOSED TO THE BEST OF THE BEST IN OUR LITTLE HOOD. I ABSOLUTELY LOVE J.H.S. 50!

KG WROTE, THEY TRANSFERRED ME TO J.H.S. 50, I GRADUATED THERE. BEST TIME I HAD IN MY LIFE, BEST SCHOOL ON THE PLANET. WORD UP IS J.H.S. 50, CHEERS AND GOD BLESS MR. EDDIE THE BEST TEACHER I HAD IN MY LIFE.
MELVA WROTE, J.H.S. 50 1976 LOVED IT. MR. MARK, AND MR. AL 2 ARE TWO OF THE 3 TEACHERS MELVA REMEMBERS. {LET'S ADD THESE ARE GREAT BUMS WHO ARE BEING REMEMBERED}

ENID WROTE, THESE WERE THE DAYS! I STILL TALK ABOUT IT! IN FACT, TEACHING MY STUDENTS YESTERDAY ABOUT HANUKKAH, I TOLD THEM I LEARNED HEBREW AT J.H.S. 50 AND LOVED IT! WE HAD THE BEST EDUCATION!

EVIE SIMPLY SAID, J.H.S. 50 IN THE 80'S WAS THE BEST.

THIS BOOK STARTED WITH THE THOUGHTS OF SOME JUNIOR HIGH SCHOOL 50 TEACHERS REMEMBERING THE CHARACTERS THAT SPENT TIME IN THE BUMS ROOM. BUT, AFTER VIEWING THE PRECIOUS MEMORIES SHOWN BY THE RESPONSES OF PAST JUNIOR HIGH SCHOOL 50 STUDENTS, THEIR THOUGHTS AND FEELINGS HAD TO BE PART OF THIS BOOK. MANY RESPONSES APPEAR IN A JUNIOR HIGH SCHOOL 50 POST BY STEVE ON DEC. 3, 2021. THE POST IS A VERY IMPORTANT PART FOR THIS BOOK. IT SHOWS THAT THE KIDS REALIZE THE OUTSTANDING, SOLID STAFF OF TEACHERS THEY HAD IN JUNIOR HIGH SCHOOL 50. THE BUMS WERE APPRECIATED BY EACH OTHER AND YEARS LATER APPRECIATED BY THEIR STUDENTS. THE BUMS WERE A SPECIAL GROUP.

HERE IT'S EMPHASIZED THAT THIRTY, FORTY, FIFTY YEARS LATER THE WRITINGS ON THE INTERNET SITE SHOWS THE STUDENTS STILL REMEMBER THEIR JUNIOR HIGH SCHOOL 50 TEACHERS. THE MEMORIES, THOUGHTS AND FEELINGS OF THE JUNIOR HIGH SCHOOL 50 STUDENTS CONCERNING THEIR TEACHERS IS SO POSITIVE. THE RESPONSES ON THE MAIN SITE AND TO THE POST QUESTIONS BELLOWS OUT FONDNESS FOR THE SCHOOL AND ITS STAFF.

USING ONLY FIRST NAMES WITH A SMEAR OF THEIR INFORMATION, HERE COMES MORE TEACHERS REMEMBERED BY THE STUDENTS.

THE POSTS SOUGHT REPONSES FROM THE JUNIOR HIGH SCHOOL 50 ALUMNI. THERE WERE POSTS LIKE J.H.S. 50 STUDENTS 1960'S TO 1990'S, THE FAVORITE DEAN POST, WHO WAS YOUR SCIENCE TEACHER POST, WHO WAS YOUR FUNNIEST TEACHER POST AND MANY OTHER POSTS ON THE JOHN D. WELLS J.H.S. 50 SITE. THESE POSTS RENDERED MANY AFFECTIONATE RESPONSES FROM THE STUDENTS. HERE ARE TEACHERS REMEMBERED BY THE STUDENTS.

NO FULL NAMES TO PROTECT THE GUILTY.

MR. GEORGE WAS REMEMBERED FOR THE PERIODIC TABLE, BOW TIE, SEATS AND DESKS SCREWED TO THE FLOOR   MR. MIKE 1, SCIENCE, A-V SQUAD   MR. BEN 1, ART TEACHER   MR. PETE 1, GYM TEACHER, G.O. COORDINATOR   MR. TIM, SCIENCE AND MATH TEACHER   MR. MARK, SCIENCE TEACHER, LUNCHROOM COORDINATOR   MR. NAT, DEAN, LUNCHROOM COORDINATOR   MR. LEONARD, TEACHER TALENT SHOW   BOSS GENE, SOCIAL STUDIES   MR. HARVEY, SOCIAL STUDIES, TRIP TO A MOVIE LEADING TO A CLASSROOM TRIAL   MR. VINNY, SOCIAL STUDIES, LUNCHROOM COORDINATOR ASSISTANT PRINCIPAL BERNIE, MR. JOE 1, SOCIAL STUDIES, READING TEACHER   MR. AL 2, SOCIAL STUDIES, QUIRKY CLOSET WITH COSTUMES   MR. ENRICO, BAND   MR. GENE, MATH   MR. SID 3, MATH   MR. SAM 1, MATH   MR. S., MATH   MR. ROBERT 1, TEACHER TALENT SHOW, GYM TEACHER   MR. EDDIE, FAVORITE TEACHER   MR. STEVE, GYM TEACHER   MR. JERRY, MATH, VACATION DAY CAMP PROGRAM

SO MANY BUMS REMEMBERED WITH RESPECT AND GRATITUDE BY THEIR FORMER STUDENTS.

ON THE JOHN D. WELLS J.H.S. 50 GROUP SITE, STUDENTS ALSO SHARED PHOTOS OF THEIR TEACHERS. ALTHOUGH THE PHOTOS DO NOT APPEAR IN THIS BOOK, THEY SHOULD BE ACKNOWLEDGED BECAUSE THE STUDENTS DISPLAYED THEM ON THE JUNIOR HIGH SCHOOL 50 SITE. MR. AL 2, SOCIAL STUDIES CHAIRMAN. MR. GEORGE, JUNIOR HIGH SCHOOL 50'S SENIOR TEACHER. MR. NAT, DEAN, LUNCHROOM COORDINATOR. MR. GENE, MATH. MR. ENRICO, BAND AND INSTRUMENTAL. MR. ROBERT 1 GYM TEACHER, SHOP TEACHER AND TEACHER TALENT SHOW. MR. ROBERT 2 BOOK CONTRIBUTOR. ASSISTANT PRINCIPAL BERNIE. MR. VINNY, SOCIAL STUDIES, LUNCHROOM COORDINATOR. BOSS GENE, SOCIAL STUDIES. MR. MIKE 1 WITH HIS AUDIO-VISUAL SQUAD. MANY PICTURES POSTED BY THE STUDENTS WERE BUMS CLUB MEMBERS.
THE JOHN D. WELLS J.H.S. 50 GROUP SITE SHOWS THAT YOU TEACHERS MADE A LASTING IMPRESSION ON YOUR STUDENTS. TEACHERS, YOU WERE EXTRAORDINARY AND REMEMBERED, TAKE A BOW!

BUMS Smiling

## A SCHOOL FOR GENERATIONS

RECOGNIZING THE FEELINGS OF THE STUDENTS FOR JUNIOR HIGH SCHOOL 50, PROMPTED THE POSTING OF THIS QUESTION, "DID ANY JUNIOR HIGH SCHOOL 50 STUDENT HAVE THEIR CHILD GO TO J.H.S. 50?". SOON CAME GENERATIONAL RESPONSES.

- LESLIE WROTE, MY MOM, MY UNCLE AND ALL MY AUNTS ATTENDED 50==SO DID ME AND MY BROTHERS==THAT'S A THREE GENERATION RESPONSE. YOLANDA YES MY MOM, MYSELF AND MY DAUGHTER, ANOTHER THREE GENERATIONAL RESPONSE
- ELIUT WROTE MY BEST FRIEND AND HIS DAUGHTER
- MARTHA WROTE YES I DID, BOTH MY DAUGHTERS, I GRADUATED IN 1977, MY DAUGHTERS IN 1997 AND 1999
- EVELYN WROTE, YES 4 OF MY 5 WENT TO 50 THEN WE MOVED TO WESTCHESTER

HERE'S ANOTHER THREE GENERATION RESPONSE:

- ALICE YES I HAD FOUR OF THEM AND 6 GRANDKIDS
- ARNOLD MY MOM AND DAD GRADUATED 50. SO DID I
- SARITA WROTE, MY BROTHER AND I WENT AS DID 2 OF HIS SONS
- MARIBEL YEA ME MY BROTHER, SISTER AND MY 3 KIDS
- LIZZETTE YES MYSELF AND MY OLDEST DAUGHTER

- JEANETTE SAID MY CHILDREN WENT TO THIS SCHOOL. THEY'RE ALL GROWN AND HAVE CHILDREN OF THEIR OWN

HERE'S ANOTHER THREE GENERATION FAMILY:
- MERCEDES WROTE WOW THAT'S CRAZY, MY 5 SONS NOW MY GRANDCHILDREN
- MARY YES, MY TWO OLDER BOYS. MR. VINNY HIT ME ON MY HEAD OPEN SCHOOL NIGHT FOR MAKING HIM FEEL OLD. MAY HE CONTINUE RESTING IN PEACE.

THERE ARE CERTAIN FEELINGS THAT COME OVER A TEACHER WHEN YOU TEACH SECOND GENERATION STUDENTS. THERE IS ONE KIND OF FEELING WHEN SEEING A STUDENT WITH A PARENT THAT WAS A RESPECTFUL STUDENT AND ANOTHER TYPE OF THOUGHT WHEN YOU SEE A STUDENT WITH A PARENT THAT WAS DISRUPTIVE AND UNCOOPERATIVE WHEN A STUDENT. THE BUMS HAVE A LITTLE FUN WHEN A PARENT THAT WAS A DISRUPTIVE STUDENT TELLS THEIR KID "RESPECT THE FUCKIN TEACHER". TO REPEAT, THIS FOUR WORD PHRASE WAS OFTEN DISPLAYED ON THE WALL OF THE BUMS ROOM, "RESPECT THE FUCKIN TEACHER"

## WILL THE BUMS HAVE A 50 YEAR REUNION?

A BUMS Birthday Party

AFTER RETIRING THERE WERE MANY MINI REUNIONS. MOSTLY TWO TO FOUR GUYS GETTING TOGETHER AT A MUSEUM, A MUSIC EVENT, A RESTAURANT OR LONG WALKS. IT'S FUN TO REPEAT WHEN VISITING A MUSEUM THAT HAD A SUGGESTED DONATION, WE WOULD DONATE A FIVE DOLLAR BILL AND SAY THIS IS FOR ALL OF US, WE ARE NEW YORKERS. MR. SID 2 TAUGHT WRITING SKILLS TO THE OFFSPRING OF SOME ACTORS AND PROMINENT PEOPLE. WHILE WALKING IN MANHATTAN, THERE WERE TIMES WE WOULD TALK TO THE DOORMEN OF BUILDINGS WHERE THESE FAMOUS PEOPLE LIVED.

ONE OF OUR MEETING PLACES WAS AT THE DONNELL LIBRARY TO HEAR THE GOTHAM JAZZMEN. A GROUP THAT PLAYED MUSIC FROM THE TWENTIES TO THE FIFTIES. A TRUMPET, A CLARINET, A TROMBONE, A PIANO, A BIG BASE AND A DRUM, EACH TAKING A SOLO ON EVERY SONG. ONE TIME WE MET AT THE DONNELL TO VIEW THE PHOTO DISPLAY BY MR. STANLEY, OUR PHOTOGRAPHER AND GREAT BUM. WHEN THE GOTHAM JAZZMEN MOVED TO THE WALTER BRUNO AUDITORIUM IN LINCOLN CENTER SOME OF US CONTINUED MEETING THERE. MINI REUNIONS TOOK US TO WEST POINT, WINERIES, ART EXHIBITS, PHOTO EXHIBITS, MUSEUMS, BEACHES, ALL BECAUSE OF OUR CONTINUED FRIENDSHIPS. THERE WERE TIMES WE HAD EIGHT OR TEN GUY GET TOGETHERS. WE MET AT ROCKEFELLER CENTER, IN CHINATOWN, IN LITTLE ITALY AND BAMONTES RESTAURANT IN WILLIAMSBURG OR IS IT GREENPOINT?

IF THE BUMS HAVE A 50 YEAR REUNION THERE WOULD BE SOME SADNESS. OF COURSE, MANY OF THE GREATEST BUMS WOULD NOT BE AT THE EVENT. THE MAIN TOPICS WOULD BE 1) REMEMBERING THE ANTICS THAT MADE EACH BUM POPULAR IN THE BUMS ROOM. 2) REMEMBERING THE STUDENTS THAT CAUSED THE MOST DIFFICULTY.

WE WOULD BE REMINDED AS WE WERE LEAVING THE BUMS ROOM, THAT WE WOULD HEAR MR. STANLEY YELLING A BATTLE CRY, WE HAVE NOT YET BEGUN TO FIGHT OR BONZAI, BONZAI. THAT'S AFTER HE ENTERED THE ROOM DOING THE MONKEY. HE LIKED JUMPING FROM THE FLOOR ONTO THE CHAIRS TO THE WINDOWSILL BEFORE SITTING DOWN. WHEN HE TRANSFERRED FROM JUNIOR HIGH SCHOOL 50 TO A SCHOOL MUCH CLOSER TO HIS HOME, MR. STANLEY

WOULD COMPARE HIS NEW TEACHERS' LOUNGE TO THE BUMS ROOM. HE WOULD SAY, YOU ONLY SEE THE TOPS OF PEOPLE'S HEADS, YOU DON'T SEE A FACE. THEY ARE PREPARING LESSONS, MARKING TESTS, WRITING LETTERS, ALWAYS BUSY. HE'D YELL, DOES ANYONE HERE KNOW HOW TO TALK?

WE WOULD TALK ABOUT USING THE EXCESS COFFEE CLUB MONEY FOR GREAT END OF MONTH LUNCHES. MR. DON WHO PROVIDED A GALLON OF HOMEMADE RED FROM HIS DAD'S WINE CELLAR BECAME A PRINCIPAL. WE WOULD LIKE TO KNOW IF THERE'S A BUMS ROOM IN HIS SCHOOL AND IF HE'S STILL BRINGING IN THE GALLON OF RED. WE WOULD LAUGH ABOUT MR. RAY NOT DRIVING TO FLORIDA IN HIS NEW CAR BECAUSE HE GOT LOST IN STATEN ISLAND, JUST 20 MINUTES FROM HIS HOUSE. HE WOULD BE ASKED IF HE'S STILL PLANNING TO DRIVE DOWN TO FLORIDA TO SEE HIS RELATIVES. MR. MARV WOULD LAY ODDS THAT HE WOULD GET LOST AGAIN. WE WOULD BE REMINDED ABOUT END OF THE MR. PETE 1, MR. AL 3 CARPOOL. DURING THE BIG GAS SHORTAGE MR. PETE 1 DROVE MR. AL 3 TO SCHOOL. IN THE BUMS ROOM MR. PETE 1 TOLD US HE HAS A FIVE GALLON CAN OF GAS IN HIS TRUNK. MR. AL 3 WENT BESERK AS HE HEARD PEOPLE SAY IF THE CAR GOT REAR ENDED IT WOULD EXPLODE INTO FLAMES. HE LET MR. PETE 1 KNOW HE'D NEVER RIDE WITH HIM AGAIN. MR. AL 3 STOPPED SPEAKING WITH MR. PETE 1. BUT THE BUMS KEPT ASKING MR. PETE 1 WHAT TIME ARE YOU PICKING UP MR. AL 3 TOMORROW?

THE MR. PETE 1 WALL DECORATIONS GOT PLENTY OF ATTENTION FROM INSIDE AND OUTSIDE THE BUMS ROOM. WE WOULD COMPLIMENT MR. PETE 1 FOR AMUSING THE TROOPS WITH HIS WALL

DECORATIONS. THE MR. LENNY 1 TANK POSTERS, THE RUSTY FENCE GATE THAT HE HUNG ON THE WALL TO SHOW OUR APPRECIATION FOR THE NEW GATES READING PROGRAM AND MY FAVORITE, THE EYE CHART USING THE LETTERS OF THE NAME OF THE NEW PRINCIPAL. THIS WAS AN ATTENTION GETTER. IT WAS A CLUE THAT THE NEW GUY WOULD NOT BE IDOLIZED BY THE BUMS. THE PREVIOUS PRINCIPAL FRANK THOUGHT GETTING ALONG WITH THIS WONDERFUL GROUP OF TEACHERS MEANT BETTER MORALE. THIS WAS SHOWN WHEN MANY OF US PARTICIPATED IN HIS PRODUCTION OF "ARSENIC AND OLD LACE".

THE NEW, EYE CHART PRINCIPAL LOOKED TO PLAY HARD BALL. AFTER HIS FIFTH YEAR AT JUNIOR HIGH SCHOOL 50, HE REPLACED THE BUMS ROOM WITH A MIMEOGRAPH ROOM. MACHINES, PAPER AND INK CROWDED THE OLD BUMS ROOM. A TEACHER AIDE WAS NOW IN THE BUMS ROOM MAKING COPIES FOR THE STAFF. THE NEW TEACHER'S LOUNGE WAS TWICE THE SIZE, HAD A VERY LARGE CLOSET, BUT NO BATHROOM. IT ACTUALLY COULD BE CALLED AN IMPROVEMENT, BUT IT DIDN'T FEEL LIKE HOME. WE MISSED THE CLOSENESS, THE LIKE HOME FEELING, THE OLD SUNKEN COT AND MAYBE THE SHMUTZ. THE ROOM AND THE LARGE CLOSET WAS THE ONE WHERE MR. AL 2 DID HIS MAGICAL TEACHING.

BUT THIS MIGHT HAVE BEEN THE DOWNFALL OF THE EYE CHART PRINCIPAL. AFTER MR. MARIO BECAME THE DISTRICT SUPERINTENDANT, THE EYE CHART PRINCIPAL SUBMITTED HIS RETIREMENT PAPERS. HE WAS REPLACED BY A MUCH MORE FRIENDLY GUY.

THE BUMS CLUB WAS ACTIVE FOR 30 YEARS, THROUGH FOUR DIFFERENT PRINCIPALS. IT WAS FORMED DURING THE TERM OF PRINCIPAL DAVID 1.

PRINCIPAL DAVID 1 WAS WELL RESPECTED FOR HIS MILITARY SERVICE AND SPENT FIVE YEARS AT JUNIOR HIGH SCHOOL 50. PRINCIPAL DAVID 1 WAS FOLLOWED BY A JUNIOR HIGH SCHOOL 50 ASSISTANT PRINCIPAL, DAVID 2, QUITE FAMILIAR WITH THE SCHOOL. MR. DAVID 2 HAD BEEN A STUDENT, AN ENGLISH TEACHER, AT JUNIOR HIGH SCHOOL 50 BEFORE BECOMING THE ASSISSTANT PRINCIPAL THEN THE PRINCIPAL. HIS PREVIOUS BACKGROUND AND CAREER OBVIOUSLY SHOWED HIM TO BE AN EDUCATOR. PRINCIPAL DAVID 2 LED JUNIOR HIGH SCHOOL 50 FOR FIVE YEARS, THEN WAS ELEVATED TO PRINCIPAL OF THE NEIGHBORHOOD ZONED HIGH SCHOOL.
WHEN MR. DAVID 2 LEFT JUNIOR HIGH SCHOOL 50, MR. FRANK, AN ASSISTANT PRINCIPAL, IN A NEIGHBORING JUNIOR HIGH SCHOOL BECAME THE NEW PRINCIPAL AT JUNIOR HIGH SCHOOL 50. HE WAS A BIT LOOSER THAN THE PREVIOUS PRINCIPALS. HE JOINED THE POKER GAMES WITH THE BUMS DURING SCHOOL HALFDAYS. HE ENJOYED THE PLACE FOR HIS FIFTEEN YEARS AS PRINCIPAL AT JUNIOR HIGH SCHOOL 50. HIS INTEREST IN BROADWAY THEATRE, GAVE HIM A FEEL FOR THE CHARACTERS THAT MADE UP THE FACULTY. ONE MORNING AS WE STOOD A FEW FEET AWAY FROM THE TIMECLOCK, PRINCIPAL FRANK LOOKED AT ME AND SAID, "SOME STRANGE DUCKS IN THIS PLACE". I SAID, YOU SAY SOME, I THEN ASKED HIM "CAN YOU NAME ONE WHO'S COMPLETELY NORMAL?" ALL IN FUN, WE WATCHED AS THE TEACHERS CLOCKED IN ONE BY ONE, DECIDING THAT THERE WAS JUST ONE PRETTY NORMAL TEACHER IN THAT GROUP. WE ALSO AGREED NEITHER OF US WOULD QUALIFY. WHEN PRINCIPAL FRANK RETIRED, HE LEFT WITH NICE FEELINGS FOR THE STAFF AND THE STAFF FOR HIM. BEST WISHES TO A GOOD BUM.

BEFORE COMING TO US, THE PRINCIPAL THAT REPLACED PRINCIPAL FRANK, WAS ALSO AN ASSISTANT PRINCIPAL, BUT WITH A COMPLETELY DIFFERENT ATTITUDE. HE HIRED ASSISTANT PRINCIPALS THAT ACTED LIKE HENCHMEN. HIS TWO ASSISTANT PRINCIPALS WERE WEIGHTLIFTERS. THEY APPROACHED YOU WITH A TOUGH GUY ATTITUDE. THE SCHOOL THEN HAD A COMPLETELY DIFFERENT ATMOSPHERE. THERE WAS A STRONG EMPHASIS ON STUDENT DISCIPLINE AND TEACHER DISCIPLINE. THIS WOULD BE A MAIN TOPIC DISCUSSED AT A BUMS 50 YEAR REUNION.

AT A BUMS REUNION, THE BUMS ROOM REFRIGERATOR WOULD BE DISCUSSED. AT SOME POINT AN OLD REFRIGERATOR WOUND UP IN THE BUMS ROOM. IT PROBABLY CAME FROM THE CHILD CARE SHOP. AT THE REUNION WE WOULD TRY TO FIGURE OUT WHO WAS THE CULPRIT THAT KEPT STEALING OTHER PEOPLE'S LUNCHES. THE LUNCH ROBBER ONLY TOOK NICELY PACKED LUNCHES. WE WOULD ALSO LIKE TO KNOW WHO NEVER ATE THE LUNCH THEY PUT IN THE REFRIGERATOR, LETTING IT ROT, CAUSING THAT DEATHLY ODOR EVERYTIME THE REFRIGERATOR DOOR WAS OPENED.
 AFTER A COUPLE OF WEEKS IN THE REFRIGERATOR, THE FOOD ROTTED CAUSING A BLAST OF STINK WHENEVER THE DOOR WAS OPENED. IT REQUIRED A GAS MASK TO BREATHE THE FUMES. THE REFRIGERATOR COULD HAVE BEEN A GOOD THING BUT IT WAS REMOVED BY BUMS REQUEST.

SMILES WOULD COME FROM THE MR. EDDIE CAPER. MR. EDDIE, A BUMS ROOM VISITOR, WAS KNOWN TO EXTEND THE HOLIDAY VACATION EVERY YEAR. VACATION TIME HE VISITED HIS UNCLE WHO LIVED IN MEXICO. AFTER THE NEW PRINCIPAL'S FIRST

YEAR, HE WARNED MR. EDDIE NOT TO EXTEND THE HOLIDAY VACATION. THEY DID SPEAK ABOUT EXTENUATING CIRCUMSTANCES. THEIR MEETING ENDED WITH WISHING EACH OTHER A GOOD HOLIDAY. WHEN THE TEACHERS RETURNED BACK TO SCHOOL, MR. EDDIE WAS NO WHERE TO BE SEEN. FIVE DAYS LATER HE CAME BACK TO WORK. HE WAS ASKED TO A MEETING IN THE PRINCIPAL'S OFFICE. AFTER HIS VISIT WITH THE PRINCIPAL, MR. EDDIE CAME INTO THE BUMS ROOM AND TOLD US THAT HE GAVE THE PRINCIPAL A MEDICAL EXCUSE LETTER FROM A TRIBAL MEDICINE MAN WRITTEN IN HIS INDIGENUOS LANGUAGE. THINK ABOUT THIS ONE. WHAT WAS THE PRINCIPAL GOING TO DO WITH A LETTER WRITTEN IN NAHUATI OR OTOMI OR MIXTECO? THERE ARE SEVEN MILLION MEXICANS SPEAKING THEIR INDIGENUOS LANGUAGE. MR. EDDIE CAME BACK FEELING WELL. WE ASKED IF THE MEDICINE MAN ACCEPTED HIS MEDICAL INSURANCE. WHEN BUMS TALK ON THE PHONE, THEY OFTEN REPEAT THE SAME CLASSROOM MEMORIES. MR. JERRY WAS ASKED TO ALLOW A NEW MATH TEACHER TO OBSERVE HIS LESSON. THE NEW TEACHER STILL TALKS ABOUT THE ANSWER GIVEN BY A STUDENT. IT WENT SOMETHING LIKE THIS. THE PRICE IS 3 FOR $1. IF YOU GET 3 FOR ONE DOLLAR, WHAT IS THE PRICE OF EACH ONE? WHEN A KID CALLED OUT 25 CENTS, WE ASCERTAINED THAT AT 25 CENTS, 3 WOULD COST 75 CENTS. MR. JERRY ASKED WHAT ABOUT THE 25 CENTS LEFTOVER? THE KID SAID, WHAT ABOUT THE TAXES? THIS NEW TEACHER, WHO WAS ALSO AN ACCOUNTANT, WOULD OFTEN SEE MR. JERRY AND SAY, "WHAT ABOUT THE TAXES?" HE GOT A KICK OUT OF IT.

IF THERE WAS A BUMS 50 YEAR REUNION, WE WOULD RECOGNIZE TEACHERS WITH SPECIAL SKILLS AND

AWARDS. MR. MEL WAS HONORED AT THE WHITE HOUSE, BRINGING HOME A MEDAL FOR HIS SKILLS IN TEACHING SCIENCE. HE WOULD GO OUT OF HIS WAY TO PURCHASE LETTUCE, CARROTS AND OTHER FOOD AT THE LOWEST COST. THE MORE HE GOT, THE MORE THE KIDS COULD PARTICIPATE WITH THE ANIMALS IN THE CLASSROOM. MR. MEL ORDERED AND DISTRIBUTED THE ORIGINAL GOLD BUM'S PINS. A GREAT BUM.

MR. SID 2 TUTORED A STUDENT HELPING HER TO WIN A NEW YORK CITY ESSAY CONTEST. MR. SID 2 ACCOMPANIED HER TO GET THE AWARD AT CITY HALL.

DEAN SAM WAS VALEDICTORIAN AT HIS UNIVERSITY GRADUATION. MANY BUMS AND BUMS ROOM VISITORS WENT ON TO BE ATTORNEYS AND SOME GUYS, MR. SAM 3, MR. MARTY 1, MR. ENRICO, MR. DON, MR. MARIO AND MR. NEFTI BECAME ADMINSTRATORS IN THE NEW YORK CITY SCHOOL SYSTEM. ALL OF THIS WOULD BE TALKED ABOUT, IF THERE WAS A BUMS 50 YEAR REUNION. THERE ARE BUMS THAT WROTE BOOKS AND BUMS THAT TAUGHT AT COLLEGES. THE BUMS WERE A SUPERB, IMPRESSIVE GROUP OF PEOPLE.

AT THE 50 YEAR REUNION, WE WOULD HAVE TO MENTION MR. LEON, A BUMS ROOM VISTOR ONLY WHEN HE NEEDED TO SNEAK A CUP OF COFFEE. THE ONE GOOD THING IS HE USUALLY HAD SMALL CONTAINERS OF MILK IN HIS SUIT JACKET POCKETS FROM THE STUDENT LUNCHROOM SO HE DIDN'T USE OUR MILK. WHEN HE WAS ADMONISHED FOR TAKING COFFEE WITHOUT JOINING THE COFFEE CLUB, HE GAVE US A FULL POCKET OF PLASTIC SPOONS GOTTEN FROM???

MR. S. ATTENDED MANY MINI REUNIONS. HE WAS A SOLID BUM. WE WOULD REMEMBER HIS HUMOR FILLED COMMENTS. THE BASEMENT OF JUNIOR HIGH SCHOOL 50 HAD THE HEATING SYSTEM, STORAGE ROOMS AND OPEN SPACES. ONE STORAGE ROOM HAD PILES OF OLD TEXTBOOKS. THE SCHOOL CUSTODIAN THOUGHT IF THEY HAVE NO USE, WHY NOT BURN THEM. MR. S. CAME UP WITH THE THOUGHT, NEXT TIME WE SHOULD ORDER TEXTBOOKS BY THE CORD.

MANY OF THE PRANKS WOULD BE REMEMBERED. PRANKS LIKE INTERCEPTING THE AUDIOVISUAL EQUIPMENT AND ONLY RETURNING THE ELECTRIC CORD TO MR. AL 3, THE DEPARTMENT CHAIRMAN. THE SOCIAL STUDIES CHAIRMAN SIGN REVERSED AND SCREWED ONTO THE DOOR UPSIDE DOWN BY TWO MEMBERS OF THE SOCIAL STUDIES DEPARTMENT. THE USE OTHER DOOR SIGN TO THE ROOM HAVING ONE DOOR. THE VICE RAID HEADLINE ABOVE THE BUMS ROOM DOOR. THE SHOPPING WAGON PLACED IN THE MAIN ENTRANCE SHOWCASE. THE RED AND WHITE CHECKERED SHIRT MADE INTO A JIGSAW PUZZLE. THE ONLY FEMALE CLUB MEMBER BECAUSE SHE PRESENTED US WITH A NEW TABLECLOTH TO COVER OUR UNSITELY TABLE. OF COURSE, THE EYE CHART WITH THE LETTERS OF THE PRINCIPALS NAME, HANGING ON THE BUMS ROOM WALL WAS REALLY A SIGHT.

SO FAR, WE HAVE NOT COMMENTED ABOUT OUR PROBLEM STUDENTS. MAYBE THE TWIN BOYS THAT LIVED ACROSS FROM THE SCHOOL WILL BE REMEMBERED. THE TWIN BOYS WERE BOTH NAMED JOSE. THERE WAS CONCERN AT DISMISSAL WHEN THEY STOOD ACROSS THE STREET OPPOSITE THE SCHOOL ENTRANCE WITH THEIR PITBULLS.

ON THE STREET CORNER ACROSS FROM THE SCHOOL, STOOD A GROUP OF GUYS. SOME HAD BATS OR GOLF CLUBS MAKING IT UNEASY FOR THE KIDS THAT HAD TO PASS THEM TO GET HOME. YEARS LATER, TWO OF THESE BOYS WENT TO ROB A LITTLE RESTAURANT WHILE TWO COPS WERE EATING THERE. IT DIDN'T GO WELL FOR THEM.

THERE WAS A TOUGH KID THAT LIKED SOMEONE'S LEATHER COAT. HE WAS ABLE TO GET A HOLD OF IT. TO GET IT OUT OF THE BUILDING, HE TALKED THIS SMALLER KID INTO WEARING THE COAT WHEN LEAVING SCHOOL. DEAN SAM LEARNED ABOUT THE STOLEN COAT SO HE WAITED OUTSIDE WITH HIS SQUAD. THEY SPOTTED THE LITTLE KID WEARING TWO COATS. IT WAS EASY TO GET THE ORIGINAL COAT STEALER. THE DEAN AND HIS DEPUTIES COULD EASILY BE A SITCOM. REMEMBER DEAN SAM'S DEPUTY RAY TRYING TO USE A WALKIE TALKIE CODE TO REPORT THE GIRL AND BOY BEHIND THE AUDITORIUM INCIDENT?

ANOTHER KID, SMALL IN STATURE, BUT ALWAYS A BIG PROBLEM WAS IN THE BOYS' BATHROOM WITH A NINTH GRADER. HE FELT IT NECESSARY TO REMOVE A PEN FROM THE NINTH GRADER'S SHIRT POCKET. WHEN HE OPENED THE DOOR TO RUN OUT WITH THE PEN, THE NINTH GRADER KICKED THE DOOR CATCHING HIS HAND AND SEVERING A PIECE OF FINGER THAT FELL TO THE FLOOR. MR. JERRY PICKED UP THE PIECE OF FINGER AND MR. GEORGE THE SCIENCE TEACHER, HEARING WHAT HAPPENED GOT ICE FROM THE LAB AND WRAPPED THE FINGER. THE KID AND THE FINGER WERE TAKEN TO THE HOSPITAL. BELIEVE IT OR NOT, NEXT DAY THE KID WAS BACK IN SCHOOL WEARING A BIG BANDAGE

LOOKING TO POKE OTHER STUDENTS WITH THE BANDAGED SEVERED FINGER.

MRS. TERESA ASKED A STUDENT TO START DOING THE WORK. BUT THE STUDENT DID NOT HAVE A PEN. SO, MRS. TERESA OFFERED THE STUDENT A PEN WHICH SHE TOOK AND IMMEDIATELY WROTE ON MRS. TERESA'S WHITE SWEATER. MRS. TERESA, A TEACHER'S AIDE, REFUSED TO REPORT THE INCIDENT. SHE SAID, NOTHING HAS HELPED AND SHE DID NOT WANT ANYMORE CONTACT WITH THE MOTHER. SHOULD THE STUDENT REPLACE THE SWEATER? SHOULD THE STUDENT BE REQUIRED TO WEAR THE INK MARKED SWEATER FOR A DAY? THIS INCIDENT CAN CAUSE LOSS OF SLEEP. WHAT SHOULD THE CONSEQUENCES BE?

WHEN BUMS ARE ON THE PHONE WITH EACH OTHER WE STILL TALK ABOUT SPECIAL STUDENTS OF THIRTY TO FIFTY YEARS AGO. LEFON, LUIS, MIRIAM, DAVID, PAULETTE, JOSE, CINDY, BRENDA, JAIME, GARY, ALEX, JEANETTE, WILDBOY AND OTHERS. IT'S FUN REMEMBERING THE STUDENT CHARACTERS THAT WE DEALT WITH DURING OUR TEACHING DAYS. THESE CONVERSATIONS THAT SPARK WONDERFUL MEMORIES OF THIRTY, FORTY, FIFTY YEARS AGO, PLUS THE MEMORIES DISPLAYED BY STUDENTS ON FACEBOOK, MAKE US THINK WE SURE HAD AN INTERESTNG TEACHING CAREER.

GARY WAS A TALL KID THAT DRESSED VERY WELL. GREAT SHOES, SHIRTS, SLACKS ALWAYS LOOKING GREAT. THERE WERE TIMES HE WOULD BE SEEN IN THE SUBWAY OR BY A TRAIN STATION AS A BLIND GUY. HE'D WEAR A HAT, DARK GLASSES, SPORTING A CANE WITH A SIGN. WOULD YOU CALL HIM

ENTERPRISING? HE WAS THE BEST DRESSED KID IN THE SCHOOL.

PAULETTE WAS DESIGNATED AS ONE OF TEN STUDENTS TO BE TAUGHT THE VIOLIN. MR. H. WAS A SYNPHONY VIOLINIST DISPERSED TO CERTAIN SCHOOLS TO TEACH DEPRIVED STUDENTS TO PLAY VIOLIN. PAULETTE AGREED TO BE AMONG THE GROUP OF HIS STUDENTS. PAULETTE WAS IN A HIGH EXPONENT CLASS. THE BETTER STUDENTS WERE PLACED IN THE 1,2 OR 3 CLASS. PAULETTE WAS IN AN 8=14 CLASS. WOULD YOU BELIEVE THAT AFTER THE THIRD SESSION, MR. H. SMASHED A VIOLIN ON PAULETTE'S HEAD. PAULETTE TOLD MR. VINNY, "MR. H. BROKES THE VIOLIN ON MY HEAD". MR. H. DID NOT RETURN TO JUNIOR HIGH SCHOOL 50.

MIRIAM WOULD ENTER THE CLASSROOM WITH PLENTY OF ENERGY, SHE WOULD SIT ON THE TEACHERS DESK WAITING FOR HER FIRST DISCIPLINE REQUEST OF THE PERIOD. ART CLASS WAS SPECIAL, SHE LIKED TO LAY ACROSS THE ART TEACHER'S DESK. MR. BEN 1. WAS HER HOMEROOM TEACHER AS WELL AS HER ART TEACHER. THEY GOT ALONG IN AN UNUSUAL WAY FOR TEACHER AND STUDENT. SHE GOT AWAY WITH THINGS THAT OTHER STUDENTS WOULD NOT THINK OF DOING. THE CLASS BEGAN WHEN MIRIAM WAS ASKED TO REMOVE HERSELF FROM THE TEACHER'S DESK.

JEANETTE COULD VERY EASILY BE DISTRACTED BY OTHER STUDENTS. SOME KNEW HOW TO SET HER OFF, CAUSING HER TO USE WORDS NOT ACCEPTABLE IN A CLASSROOM. GETTING HER ATTENTION WAS A GAME SOME KIDS PLAYED. THEY KNEW SHE WOULD LET LOOSE WITH SOME OF HER FAVORITE WORDS. SHE WOULD ERUPT AND DISRUPT THE CLASS. THIS

CAUSED A TEACHER TO REQUEST HER MOTHER TO COME UP TO THE SCHOOL. AFTER THE TEACHER EXPLAINED HER DAUGHTER'S OUTBURSTS AND THE WORDS USED. THE MOM JUST SAID. "SHE DOES THAT AT HOME TOO". JEANETTE JUST KEPT BEING JEANETTE.

JAMES WAS NOT YET 15 YEARS OLD WHEN HE HAD A GUN TO DO A ROBBERY. BECAUSE OF HIS AGE THE SYSTEM HAD HIM TRANSFERRED TO A NEIGHBORING SCHOOL SO HE SHOULDN'T MISS OUT ON HIS EDUCATION. WITH THREE MONTHS OF SATISFACTORY ATTENDANCE AND BEHAVIOR AT HIS NEW SCHOOL, JAMES COULD RETURN TO JUNIOR HIGH SCHOOL 50 WHICH WAS CLOSER TO HIS HOME. SO, THREE MONTHS LATER THE PRINCIPAL RATED JAMES SATISFACTORY. WAS THE PRINCIPAL SORRY TO SEE JAMES LEAVE HIS SCHOOL? JAMES' AUNT TOLD US SHE WAS AFRAID WHEN JAMES CAME TO HER HOUSE. SHE HAD TO HIDE HER MONEY.

WHEN CERTAIN BOYS ASK TO GO TO THE BATHROOM IT'S A HAPPY MOMENT FOR THE TEACHER. LUIS WAS ONE OF THOSE BOYS. ONE DAY, THE PRINCIPAL, WHILE TOURING THE BUILDING OBSERVED LUIS STROLLING DOWN THE HALL, LOOKING INTO EACH CLASSROOM. THE PRINCIPAL ASCERTAINED THAT LUIS HAD A BATHROOM PASS BUT WAS NOT ON THE PROPER FLOOR.
THE PRINCIPAL ASKED LUIS TO BRING HIS MOTHER TO SCHOOL IN THE MORNING.
LUIS SAID, "I DON'T HAVE A MOTHER".
THE PRINCIPAL ASKED, "WHO DO YOU LIVE WITH?"
LUIS SAID, "MY SISTER"
THE PRINCIPAL SAID, "BRING HER UP TOMORROW MORNING"
LUIS SAID, "WHO'S GOING TO WATCH HER BABIES?"

THE PRINCIPAL SAID, "SHE CAN BRING THE BABIES WITH HER"

LUIS WAS BROUGHT BACK TO CLASS LOOKING FORWARD TO GET ANOTHER BATHROOM PASS FROM HIS NEXT TEACHER TO ROAM THE HALLS OF JUNIOR HIGH SCHOOL 50. BE ALERTED THAT LUIS DID NOT LIVE WITH AN OLDER SISTER WITH BABIES. SOME YEARS LATER A TEACHER ON JURY DUTY HEARD HIS NAME CALLED. IT WAS LUIS BEING ESCORTED BY COURT POLICE OFFICERS. MAYBE HE WAS BEING ESCORTED TO THE BATHROOM.

BRENDA WAS KNOWN TO SLEEP WITH HER HEAD ON HER DESK. NO STUDENT WANTED TO BE THE ONE TO WAKE HER. QUIET IN A CLASSROOM IS NICE. HOW ABOUT THIS. WHEN BRENDA WAS AWAKE, SHE MADE IT KNOWN THAT SHE WANTED TO HEAR THE TEACHER. THERE WAS NOT ONE GIRL OR BOY THAT WOULD CHALLENGE HER. ALL WERE QUIET. TEACHERS DID NOT WANT TO CHALLENGE HER. WHEN BRENDA WAS IN SCHOOL THE CLASS WAS QUIET WHETHER SHE SLEPT OR WAS AWAKE.

JAIME WOULD NOT PUT HIS COAT IN THE WARDROBE DURING MORNING HOMEROOM. STUDENTS HANG THEIR COATS ON A HOOK IN THE WARDROBE THAT IS LOCKED UNTIL THE AFTERNOON DISMISSAL. JAIME HAD A DIFFERENT IDEA ABOUT HIS COAT. HE WANTED TO WEAR HIS LONG DARK OVERCOAT ALL DAY. HIS COAT WAS A HEAVYWEIGHT COAT THAT REACHED DOWN TO HIS ANKLES. THERE WERE DAYS HE WORE IT IN THE CLASSROOMS, IN THE AUDITORIUM, IN THE LUNCHROOM AND EVEN IN THE GYM. IT MIGHT BE CALLED A SECURITY BLANKET. A STAFF MEMBER WOULD NOT REMOVE IT FORCIBLY.

AN ADMINISTRATOR WOULD THINK TWICE BEFORE SENDING A STUDENT HOME, TO MISS SCHOOL. THE ISSUE WAS GREAT FOR DISCUSSION. IS HE HURTING ANYONE? IS THERE ANYTHING IN THE DRESS CODE LIMITING THE LAYERS OF CLOTHING? THERE WERE SOME STUDENTS THAT STAFF MEMBERS WANTED TO SEND HOME FOR WEARING "TOO LITTLE CLOTHING". I STILL HAVE A PICTURE IN MY MIND OF JAIME, A SHORT GUY, WITH HIS SHAVED HEAD AND LONG DARK OVERCOAT.

ALEX WAS A VERY BIG JUNIOR HIGH SCHOOL STUDENT. HE WAS ON THE SOCCER TEAM FOR THE COUPLE OF YEARS THAT IT EXISTED. THE USUAL SOCCER TEAM POSITIONS ARE STRIKER, MIDFIELDER, DEFENDER AND GOALIE. ALEX WAS A BOUNCER. HE WAS A BOUNCER ON THE SOCCER FIELD AS WELL AS A BOUNCER IN THE SCHOOL. HE WENT ON TO HIGH SCHOOL WHERE HE FIT IN BETTER, SIZE WISE. YEARS LATER, IN THE SUMMER HIS NEPHEW WAS EJECTED FROM THE JUNIOR HIGH SCHOOL 50 VACATION DAY CAMP. ALEX ACCOMPANIED THE KID BACK TO THE SCHOOL ASKING WHAT HAPPENED? AFTER ALL WAS EXPLAINED, IT ENDED WITH ALEX TELLING HIS NEPHEW, "RESPECT THE FUCKIN TEACHER"

WILDBOY WAS PART OF THE DEAN'S SQUAD. HE LIKED TO BE WITH DEAN SAM. EVEN THOUGH HE DID NOT ATTEND J.H.S. 50 ANYMORE. HE WOULD BE A MONITOR/GO=GETTER FOR THE DEAN. IN THE SUMMER WILDBOY WAS THE ASSISTANT COACH OF THE SOFTBALL TEAM. HE SET THE POSITIONS AND THE BATTING LINE=UP. FOR SOME REASON THE PLAYERS LISTENED TO EVERY WORD HE SAID. HAVING WILDBOY AROUND SHOWED LEADERSHIP FOR THE KIDS AND MEANT SECURITY FOR THE TEACHERS' CARS.

HERE'S A CUTE STORY FOR THE BUMS REUNION. OPEN SCHOOL NIGHTS DID NOT DRAW BIG CROWDS AT JUNIOR HIGH SCHOOL 50. IT GAVE MR. AL 1 AN OPPORTUNITY TO GET A LITTLE SLEEP AT HIS DESK. A STUDENT WOKE HIM WHEN HE LOOKED INTO THE ROOM. MR. AL 1 JUMPED UP, WENT TO THE DOOR AND ASKED THE STUDENT AND THE WOMAN WITH HIM TO COME IN TO HAVE A CONFERENCE. AFTER FIVE MINUTES OF CONFERENCING, THE STUDENT SAID "THIS IS NOT MY MOTHER".

## THE SUMMARY

THE LAST PART OF THIS BOOK WILL BE IN THE FORM OF A CLASS LESSON. THE LESSON BEGINS WITH THE MOTIVATION, LEADING TO THE MATERIAL TO BE COMMUNICATED, TO BE LEARNED. PIVOTAL QUESTIONS AND THE SUMMARY REINFORCES THE LESSON.

I WAS MOTIVATED TO WRITE THIS BOOK WHEN TALKING TO MY JUNIOR HIGH SCHOOL 50 COLLEAGUES AND FRIENDS WHO WERE ASTONISHED AT THE THINGS THAT TOOK PLACE AT MY SCHOOL. EVERYONE THOUGHT THE STORIES ABOUT MY COLLEAGUES AND THEIR ANTICS WERE INTERESTING, FUNNY AND UNEXPECTED IN ANY SCHOOL.

SO "THE BUMS CLUB" WAS PUT INTO MOTION. THE SHORT DESCRIPTION OF THE ROOM WHERE IT ALL STARTED, HOW THE THIRTY PLUS GUYS DEVELOPED INTO "THE BUMS CLUB", THE NEIGHBORHOOD AND THE STUDENT AND TEACHER MEMORIES THIRTY TO FIFTY YEARS LATER, PROVIDES THE MATERIAL THAT ANSWERS THE FOLLOWING QUESTIONS.

WHAT WAS THE PURPOSE OF THE BUMS CLUB?
WAS IT IN OTHER SCHOOLS?
WHY WOULD TEACHERS WANT TO BE CALLED BUMS?
WHAT KIND OF PRANKS AND ANTICS TOOK PLACE IN THE SCHOOL AND IN THE BUMS ROOM?
WHAT KIND OF CHARACTERS WERE IN THIS CLUB?
WHICH TEACHERS COULD BE IN A SITCOM?
WHAT WAS THE AREA AROUND THIS SCHOOL?
WHAT WILL WE HEAR FROM THE STUDENTS?
WILL WE KNOW THE THOUGHTS AND FEELINGS OF THE STUDENTS AND STAFF?

ALL OF THESE QUESTIONS ARE ANSWERED IN THE ONE HUNDRED THIRTY PLUS PAGES OF THE BOOK. THE BUMS WERE A DIVERSE GROUP OF GUYS GATHERED IN A TEACHERS ROOM THAT WAS VERY DIFFERENT THAN THE USUAL TEACHERS' LOUNGE. AMAZING IS THE NUMBER OF TEACHERS WHO COMMENTED HOW CATHARTIC IT WAS AFTER ENTERING THE BUMS ROOM. SOME SAID IT TOOK YOU AWAY FROM THE REALITIES OF LIFE. THE ATMOSPHERE WAS LIKE YOU WERE A GROUP OF GUYS HANGING OUT ON THE STREETS OF BROOKLYN. MANY TEACHERS LOOKED FORWARD TO BEING IN THAT ROOM EVERYDAY. THE BOOK WRITES ABOUT THIRTY=THREE BUMS CLUB MEMBERS, BUT THERE WERE MANY MORE BUMS THAT COULD HAVE BEEN IN THIS BOOK. WHEN TEACHERS LEFT JUNIOR HIGH SCHOOL 50 AND SPOKE ABOUT THEIR NEW SUROUNDINGS THEY WOULD COMMENT, THERE WAS NO PLACE LIKE THE BUMS ROOM. MANY WHO STAYED IN TEACHING WOULD ADD, THE TEACHING STAFF AT JUNIOR HIGH SCHOOL 50 WAS THE BEST STAFF OF TEACHERS BY FAR.

THERE WERE MANY WHO TRIED TEACHING THAT COULD NOT LAST A COUPLE OF YEARS OR EVEN SIX MONTHS. MANY COULD NOT RELATE TO THE KIDS OR ATTAIN CLASS DISCIPLINE. IT DIDN'T MATTER THE TEACHER'S SIZE. THERE WERE MALE TEACHERS WELL OVER SIX FEET TALL WHOSE CLASSES WERE OUT OF CONTROL. JUNIOR HIGH SCHOOL 50 HAD A NUMBER OF TEACHERS SMALL IN STATURE THAT EXHIBITED GREAT CLASSROOM DISCIPLINE. THE BUMS WERE A SPECIAL GROUP. SOME OF OUR TEACHERS COULD FALL ASLEEP AT THEIR DESK AND AS THE SAYING GOES, YOU COULD HEAR A PIN DROP. AT TIMES A COUPLE OF BUMS WOULD QUIETLY REMOVE THE CLASS WHILE THE TEACHER WAS

SLEEPING. SOME NEWER TEACHERS THAT WALKED PAST A SLEEPING TEACHER'S ROOM, WOULD SAY, HE HAS BETTER CONTROL SLEEPING THAN I HAVE WHEN I'M TEACHING.

GROUP 1 ANSWERS THE KIND OF CHARACTERS IN THE BUMS CLUB. A BUNCH OF REGULAR GUYS. SO, WHEN MR. AL 2 HUNG HIS MR. AL 2 SOCIAL STUDIES CHAIRMAN SIGN ON HIS CLASSROOM DOOR, MR. VINNIE AND BOSS GENE REMOVED IT AND SCREWED IT ON THE DOOR UPSIDE DOWN. THE EXTENSION CORD PRANK, THE COVERAGE SLIP PRANK AND THE DODGE THE ASSISTANT PRINCIPAL GAME ARE THE ANTICS THAT MADE THE BUMS ROOM GROUP DIFFERENT AND ENTERTAINING. SO DIFFERENT THAT THE DISTRICT SUPERINTENDANT REQUESTED MEMBERSHIP IN THIS UNUSUAL TEACHER CLUB.

GROUP 2 ANSWERS DID BUMS GET SPECIAL TREATMENT FROM THE DISTRICT OFFICE. MR. MARIO TOLD MR. STANLEY JUST WRITE ANYTHING, YOU WILL GET THE SABATICAL. MR. MARIO ADMINISTERED THE NO CONSEQUENCES PENALTY TO MR. SAM 1 FOR HIS HUGGING EPISODE. MR. MARIO APPOINTED MR. JERRY TO RECEIVE THE COUNSELOR AWARD AT THE BOARD OF EDUCATION, EVEN THOUGH THERE WERE MANY MORE EXPERIENCED COUNSELORS IN THE DISTRICT. WHEN MR. BEN 1 WAS REQUESTED TO APPEAR AT THE DISTRICT OFFICE FOR TURNING OVER A SECRETARY'S DESK, HE WAS TOLD TRY NOT TO DO IT AGAIN. MAYBE BEING A BUMS CLUB MEMBER DID GET SPECIAL TREATMENT FROM THOSE WITH INFLUENCE AT THE DISTRICT OFFICE.

THE SITCOM IDEA WOULD FOCUS ON THE BUMS ROOM CHARACTERS BUT COULD EXTEND TO THE OUR PRINCIPAL AND THE DISTRICT OFFICE. THOSE

MILITARY SITCOMS HAD PRIVATES, THE SARGEANT, THE LIEUTENANT AND THE GENERAL. THE BUMS ROOM HAD A TREASURE CHEST OF PERSONALITIES. PERSONALITIES FOR ANY KIND OF SITCOM. THERE WERE PRANKSTERS, SLEEPERS, VICTIMS, TOUGH GUYS, GRUMPY GUYS, BRAINIACS, CONTRARIANS, BOSSES, GAMBLERS, INSTIGATERS, NON= CONFORMISTS, OPTIMISTS AND PESSIMISTS. THE ROOM WAS LIVELY, INTERESTING AND FUN. OVER THE YEARS MANY TEACHERS PASSED THROUGH THE BUMS ROOM DOOR. THEY CAME IN BECAUSE OF THE ATMOSPHERE IN THAT UNORTHODOX TEACHERS' ROOM. THE BUMS PUT ON A SHOW EVERYDAY.

THE BOOK TRIES TO SHOW THE ECONOMIC LEVEL OF THE FAMILIES LIVING IN THE NEIGHBORHOOD. BASICALLY, MOM AND POP STORES, NO TENNIS COURTS, NO BASEBALL DIAMONDS, NO GRASSY PARK AREAS, NO DETATCHED ONE FAMILY HOMES, IT WAS AN INNERCITY NEIGHBORHOOD.

THE STUDENTS DISCLOSED THEIR THOUGHTS AND FEELINGS OF THE SCHOOL ON THEIR FACEBOOK "WELLS JUNIOR HIGH SCHOOL J.H.S. 50" GROUP SITE OR JOHN D. WELLS J.H.S. 50 GROUP SITE. THE RESPONSES TO THE POSTS SHOWED THEY HAVE WONDERFUL, SENTIMENTAL MEMORIES OF JUNIOR HIGH SCHOOL 50 SO MANY YEARS LATER. SO MANY REMEMBER THE NAMES OF THEIR TEACHERS OF THIRTY, FORTY AND FIFTY YEARS AGO. PEOPLE TALK ABOUT THE PEOPLE WHO MADE AN IMPRESSION ON THEM WHEN THEY WERE YOUNG. THE BUMS OBVIOUSLY MADE A LASTING IMPRESSION ON THEIR STUDENTS.

THEN THERE ARE STUDENTS THAT MADE A LASTING IMPRESSION ON THE TEACHERS. IN THE LAST PART

OF THIS BOOK, I WROTE ABOUT SOME "LASTING IMPRESSION STUDENTS". FOR SURE THERE ARE MORE THAT CAN BE INCLUDED IN THIS BOOK. WE ALL SEEK ATTENTION. PEOPLE GET ATTENTION BY DOING SOMETHING ESPECIALLY GOOD OR SOMETHING THAT'S UNEXPECTED. OFTEN THE STUDENTS REMEMBERED THE MOST ARE THE ONES THAT GO OFF THE TRACK.

THE THEME OF THIS BOOK IS REMEMBERING. IT'S REMEMBERING THE SECOND FLOOR TEACHERS' LOUNGE WHERE THE NEW GROUP OF TEACHERS GATHERED. IT'S REMEMBERING SOME STUDENTS TELLING THEIR PARENTS THAT BUMS WERE LIVING IN A ROOM ON THE SECOND FLOOR. THE ROOM WAS GIVEN THE NAME THE BUMS ROOM AND THE TEACHERS WERE HAPPY TO BE CALLED THE BUMS. THE MEMORIES OF THE GUYS IN THE BUMS CLUB CONTINUES TO GIVE US ENJOYABLE CONVERSATION AND LAUGHS.

WE STILL REMEMBER THE NEIGHBORHOOD AND THE STORES OF THE AREA. WE WERE AFFORDED A GREAT ASSORTMENT OF INTERESTING FOODS. WE WERE TREATED WONDERFULLY BY SO MANY MERCHANTS. ACORN DISTRIBUTOR OF PRETZELS, CHIPS AND OTHER SNACKS, VITA FISH, EMPIRE NATIONAL MEATS, THE PASTRAMI KING, SOL AND NICK AND MANY EXCELLENT BAKERIES OF BREADS AND CAKES.

NOT OFTEN DO WE TALK ABOUT THE PROGRAMS THAT WERE OFFERED AT JUNIOR HIGH SCHOOL 50. THEY WERE BENEFICIAL TO THOSE WHO PARTICIPATED IN THEM.
MOSTLY OUR CONVERSATIONS FOCUS ON THE INDIVIDUAL BUMS. EACH ONE OFFERED SOMETHING TO THE MENAGERIE. BOOKS HAVE A TABLE OF

CONTENTS. THIS BOOK ALSO HAS A TABLE OF BUMS CONTENT. IF YOU WANT TO REREAD ABOUT A BUM'S PRANK OR EVENT, THE TABLE OF BUMS CONTENT CAN BE HELPFUL.

THE BUMS WERE A GROUP OF PROFESSIONALS ENJOYING A PLEASANT ENVIRONMENT WHILE ACCOMPLISHING THEIR JOB. ONE OF MY FAVORITE PARTS OF THIS BOOK IS THAT THIRTY, FORTY, FIFTY YEARS AFTER THE STUDENTS LEFT JUNIOR HIGH SCHOOL 50, THEY STILL REMEMBER THE SCHOOL AND THEIR TEACHERS. WHAT A TRIBUTE TO THIS GROUP OF TEACHERS!
ON ANOTHER SIDE THE TEACHERS STILL REMEMBER AND TALK ABOUT MANY EVENTS THAT INVOLVED THEIR COLLEAGUES SO MANY YEARS AGO. THESE ARE THE STORIES AND EVENTS THAT MADE THE BUMS INTERESTING AND ENTERTAINING.
THE ROBBER CHAINED IN THE BASEMENT=
THE HOT CHERRY PEPPER BETTING EVENT=
THE PRINCIPAL EYE CHART=
THE VICE RAID HEADLINE=
THE TIE BURNING CEREMONY=
BLOOD EXTRACTED IN THE BUMS ROOM=
REMOVING A CLASS WHILE THE TEACHER IS SLEEPING=
CARRYING THE ASSISTANT PRINCIPAL UP THE STAIRS=
THE MEDICAL EXCUSE WRITTEN BY A MEDICINE MAN=
THE HALFDAY POKER GAMES=
THE TABLECLOTH INDUCTION CEREMONY FOR THE ONLY FEMALE BUM=
THE SHOPPING WAGON PUT IN THE MAIN ENTRANCE SHOWCASE=

ANOTHER FAVORITE PART IS REMEMBERING STUDENTS THAT WERE OFTEN OFF THE REGULAR TRACK. A GROUP OF THESE STUDENTS ARE IN THIS BOOK.
THE BEST DRESSED KID=
THE KID WITH HIS LONG, DARK OVERCOAT=
THE END OF THE VIOLIN LESSONS=
THE STUDENT=PRINCIPAL CONVERSATION IN THE HALL=
WHEN SHE SLEEPS THE CLASS IS QUIET=
SHE LIKED TO SIT ON THE TEACHER'S DESK=
SHE TALKS LIKE THAT AT HOME=
HE POKED KIDS WITH A BANDAGED SEVERED FINGER=
SHE TOLD THE TEACHER TO LOOK AT HER MOTHER'S BEHIND=
HE TOLD HIS NEPHEW "RESPECT THE FUCKIN TEACHER"

THANKS TO ALL THE BUMS WHO MADE THE BUMS ROOM SO INTERESTING AND ENTERTAINING. OVER THE YEARS IT WAS A PRIVILEDGE TO BE WITH THIS GROUP OF PROFESSIONALS. KNOWING MR. ROBERT 2, MR. STANLEY AND MR. S. FOR MORE THAN 50 YEARS WAS ALWAYS AN ENTERTAINING AND A LEARNING EXPERIENCE. I THANK THEM FOR THEIR MEMORIES AND MOTIVATION TO WRITE THIS BOOK.

AT THE BEGINNING OF THIS BOOK MANY TEACHERS SAID A BOOK SHOULD BE WRITTEN BUT WHO'S GONNA BELIEVE IT! IT WAS LOTS OF FUN WRITING THIS BOOK. SOMETIMES I DON'T BELIEVE IT. THE HOPE IS THAT YOU HAVE FUN READING "THE BUMS CLUB". DO YOU BELIEVE IT?

BUMS Support

MANY THANKS TO:

BARRY, ALLAN, STANLEY, LEON, AARON, STEVIE, GLENN, JOEL, JOEY, RICHIE, FRANKIE, JAMES, ROBERT, MARVIN, LARRY, DONNY, MIKE, MEL, RHODA, LANA, IDA, LYNDA, ALICIA, PHYLLIS, CARL AND SO MANY MORE.

THIS BOOK IS DEDCICATED TO THOSE KIDS THAT TOOK ADVANTAGE OF THE PHYSICAL HEALTH PROGRAM THEY RECEIVED BY WALKING TO JUNIOR HIGH SCHOOL 50, THEN GETTING THE EDUCATION THEY RECEIVED AS STUDENTS OF JUNIOR HIGH SCHOOL 50. SO, THE RESULT WAS A GROUP OF STUDENTS WITH A GOOD SET OF LEGS AND AN EDUCATION THAT PREPARED THEM TO HAVE A SUCCESSFUL FUTURE.

ALSO DEDICATED TO BOSS GENE, MR. S., MR. ROBERT 2, AND MR. STANLEY WHO CONVERSATED AND CONTRIBUTED IDEAS FOR THIS BOOK. TO DANIELLE FOR PUTTING THE BOOK TOGETHER AND TO RHODA, ANNIE, CRAIG AND LARRY FOR SMILING THE MANY TIMES THEY HEARD THE BUMS ROOM STORIES. WHY NOT ADD THE REST OF MY FAMILY, AMANDA, ARACELIS, CECILIA, ETHAN, JACOB AND LUCAS. THIS BOOK IS ALSO DEDICATED TO THOSE THAT NEED LARGE FONT IN BOOKS.

ABOUT THE AUTHOR

PUBLIC SCHOOL 16—WILLIAMSBURG, BROOKLYN

BALL PLAYING===
PUNCHBALL=STICKBALL=TRIANGLE=BOXBALL=
SOFTBALL=HARDBALL=FOOTBALL=BASKETBALL=
STOOPBASE

STREET GAMES===
RINGO LEVIO=HIDE AND SEEK=JOHNNY ON THE PONY=KICK THE CAN=BASEBALL CARD FLIPPING=COIN TOSSING=3 FEET TO??????

BOYS HIGH SCHOOL==BROOKLYN COLLEGE, B.A.==LONG ISLAND UNIVERSITY M.S.

CLUBROOMS===
KEAP ST.==RODNEY ST.==BROADWAY==SOUTH 4$^{TH}$ ST.

CATALINAS RECORDING GROUP==GLORY RECORDS "MARLENE"==WCBS FM
CATALINAS CD, "A WALK THROUGH TIME"=="LOVE IS A WONDERFUL THING"

U.S. ARMY==NEW YORK STATE ARMY NATIONAL GUARD

VOLUNTEER AMBULANCE CORP.==EMT

BOOKS WRITTEN==
"GAMES OF SATISFACTION"
"101 CARTOONS BIRDTOONS NEWSTOONS P.C."
"THE BUMS CLUB"

www.ingramcontent.com/pod-product-compliance
Lightning Source LLC
Chambersburg PA
CBHW072210070526
44585CB00015B/1276